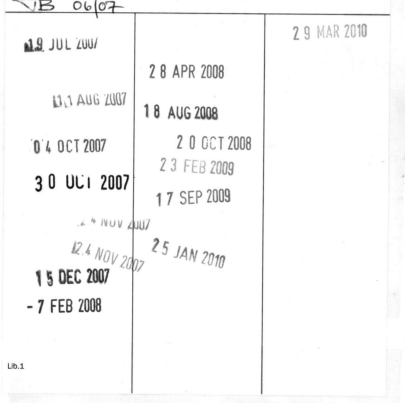

High impact CVs

New Edition

52 brilliant ideas for making your
résumé sensational

John Middleton

brilliantideas

First published in 2005, second edition 2007 by
The Infinite Ideas Company Limited
36 St Giles
Oxford
OX1 3LD
United Kingdom
www.infideas.com

A CIP catalogue record for this book is available from the British Library.

ISBN 978-1-905940-11-0

Designed and typeset by Baseline Arts Ltd, Oxford
Printed and bound in India

Brilliant ideas

Brilliant features

Each chapter of this book is designed to provide you with an inspirational idea that you can read quickly and put into practice straight away.

Throughout you'll find four features that will help you to get right to the heart of the idea:

- *Try another idea* If this idea looks like a life-changer then there's no time to lose. *Try another idea* will point you straight to a related tip to expand and enhance the first.

- *Here's an idea for you* Give it a go – right here, right now – and get an idea of how well you're doing so far.

- *Defining ideas* Words of wisdom from masters and mistresses of the art, plus some interesting hangers-on.

- *How did it go?* If at first you do succeed try to hide your amazement. If, on the other hand, you don't this is where you'll find a Q and A that highlights common problems and how to get over them.

Introduction

Question: Who's more likely to be invited to an interview? An outstanding performer with an average CV or an average performer with an outstanding CV?

When you're going for a new job, you might well be in competition with hundreds of other people. It's therefore vital for your CV to distinguish itself from the rest of the pack.

Could you convince a complete stranger that you're worth interviewing when all you have at your disposal are around 850 words and two sides of A4? Only that's the challenge for anyone looking to change jobs – to use the highly stylised and conservative format of a CV to sell ourselves.

This is harder than it sounds. I've read literally tens of thousands of CVs in my time and most of them were mind-numbingly, teeth-grindingly dull. The vast majority of CVs in circulation today make ditchwater seem comparatively interesting and redefine watching paint dry as an extreme sport for adrenalin junkies.

It's a curious thing, but when it comes to describing ourselves on paper, perfectly competent and interesting people with excellent career track records somehow manage to portray themselves as bland nonentities. To put it politely, most people have uncompelling CVs. Only a handful of us have sussed that a CV is a one-to-one marketing document, not a desiccated litany of turgid facts. But let's face it, whichever of the two camps we fall into, there's room for improvement.

And that's where this book comes in. In a nutshell, *High Impact CVs* looks at the principles and techniques involved in putting together a CV that will market you successfully rather than bore the pants off the decision makers. Look on this book as a series of prods and prompts that add up to a comprehensive CV health check. Some of the 52 ideas are action-oriented. Others are more reflective. All are designed to get you thinking about how you can improve the positive impact of your CV.

OK, that's enough preamble. Let's get going.

1

Dream a little dream

High impact CVs reflect precisely what you're looking to achieve from your career. So, before putting pen to paper, consider what you want from the work you do.

As a child, what did you want to be when you grew up? Moreover, how do you presently feel about your career? Is it moving along nicely? Going well but not well enough? Stalled?

Here are twelve questions that are designed to help you get a handle on the state of your career. Don't feel you have to answer each question in painstaking detail, simply go for those that seem the most relevant or intriguing:

1. In what elements of your career have you been most successful? And least successful?

2. What aspects of your career have you enjoyed the most? And the least?

3. More specifically, which has been the most satisfying role you have undertaken to date?

Make a list of the constraints affecting your career choices over the next few years. These may include financial issues, qualifications, where you live and work, your ability to relocate, and so on. Make a brief note of how important each constraint is.

4. With the benefit of twenty–twenty hindsight, are there any points in your career or life where you would have made a different choice or decision?

5. How do you feel when you get up to go to work in the morning?

6. What aspects of your current job do you enjoy the most? And the least?

7. Do you enjoy working with others?

8. How are you regarded by the people you work with?

9. Do subordinates, peers and senior managers hold different views about you? If so, what conclusions can you draw from this?

10. Have you had a new boss recently, say, in the last two years? If so, what impact has this had on the way you feel?

11. How ambitious are you these days?

12. What do you want out of the work you do? Are you getting it?

THE BIG THREE CAREER OPTIONS

Unless you're keen to retire, downshift, start your own business or continue as you are (in which case why are you reading this book?), here are your three main career options:

New role in the same organisation

Internal career development can be an excellent way of moving into new fields and learning new skills. Because this option involves staying in your current organisation, you wouldn't have the distraction of having to absorb a new culture or a different set of operating principles. You would also know who's who. If you're unhappy with your current work discipline, this can be a good way for you to find a more suitable area.

Similar role in a new organisation

This is perhaps the easiest proposition to take to the external job marketplace, as employers tend to be fairly conservative when assessing who they want to join their company. If they're looking for a Finance Director and you're already the Finance Director of a similar enterprise, you're much more likely to succeed than a Finance Manager from a completely different sector who's looking for a promotion.

If you're raring to crack on, turn to IDEA 2, *Remember, remember*. If, however, you're unsure whether a corporate career is for you, have a look at IDEA 50, *Do you need a CV at all?*

Try another idea...

Defining idea...

'*Optimism is a strategy for making a better future. Because unless you believe that the future can be better, it's unlikely you will step up and take responsibility for making it so. If you assume that there is no hope, you guarantee that there will be no hope.*'
NOAM CHOMSKY, quoted in *Wired*

'Ah, there's nothing more exciting than science. You get all the fun of sitting still, being quiet, writing down numbers, paying attention. Science has it all.'
PRINCIPAL SEYMOUR SKINNER, from *The Simpsons*

New role in a new organisation

Hard on the heels of the easiest proposition to take to the external job marketplace is the hardest proposition. It *is* possible to change career direction and companies at the same time, but you'll need to work hard at it and be very convincing and persuasive about (a) why you're trying to make the move and (b) your ability to perform the new role effectively.

PAUSE FOR THOUGHT

Taking stock of your career is not a five-minute exercise. Neither is deciding what you want to do next. So, let's imagine we can hear a number of harp arpeggios with reverb to denote the passage of time...

ENLIGHTENMENT

I take it you've decided what you want to do next and you're going to need a CV? Excellent. Now let's get going.

Q **I've been examining my career, but I'm struggling with the self-examination. Why should I bother?**

How did it go?

A *You're not alone. Most of us never get round to asking ourselves some fairly fundamental questions about the work we do and whether we've found our niche. Taking stock of our career to date is important, however, because it'll point to how content we currently are and whether we need to take some form of remedial action.*

Q **I can cope with looking back over my career because at least there's something concrete to explore, but how can I get to grips with questions like 'What do you want out of the work you do? Are you getting it?'**

A *To give some shape to your thinking, you may find it helpful to note what you want under the following ten headings:*

1. *Money: e.g. how much are you looking to earn?*

2. *Working hours: e.g. how many would you like to work? Nine to five or non-standard? How much holiday would you like?*

3. *Job security: e.g. how important is it to you?*

4. *Level of challenge: e.g. do you prefer to operate within a comfort zone or to be really stretched?*

5. *Type of work: e.g. manual or knowledge-based?*

5

6. **Independence**: e.g. working with other people or alone?

7. **Management responsibility**: do you welcome or hate it?

8. **Technical competence**: do you have or would you like a specialist skill?

9. **Work–life balance**: how important is it? Considering downshifting?

10. **Location**: e.g. indoors or outdoors? City or country? This country or abroad?

You should have a much better picture of your career aspirations once you've gathered your thoughts under these headings.

2

Remember, remember

Take a trip down memory lane and use the past as your starting point for a brand new CV.

Not so long ago, job applications involved little more than updating your old CV. These days, however, you'll need to take the time to create a brand spanking new one from scratch in order to be up there with the best of 'em.

Remember how it used to be in days gone by when we decided the time had come to change jobs? When an advert caught our eye, we simply dug out a copy of the CV we used when we last applied for a job, checked that we were still living at the same address, added in details of our latest role and maybe topped up the qualification section if we'd been studying. Then it was off to the office photocopier to surreptitiously get a whole bunch of copies ready to send off for that particular job and any others that took our fancy. If you were at the more sophisticated end of the market, you might have taken the time to compose a covering letter to attach to your CV, but that was about it.

Here's an idea for you... **As soon as you take on a new role or responsibility, add this to your basic CV. And whenever you remember further information about earlier roles, make sure you add this to your master document too.**

Aside from any effort involved in getting the application to the nearest postbox, it was generally a low-energy exercise. But like the cricketer who used to have a pint and a cigarette between innings has become an outdated sporting phenomenon, so has the amateur applicant been consigned to the corporate dustbin of history.

BE UPFRONT AND PERSONAL

CVs have gone professional and also very, very personal. They used to be about job descriptions and duties; now they zone in on achievements and what we as individuals bring to the corporate party.

Putting together a CV that will succeed in the 21st-century job market will require time and effort. Your CV will need to be relevant and to the point. You'll be fighting a lost cause if you rely on the recipient spending their precious time on sifting through your CV to locate the information they're particularly interested in. A one-way ticket to the reject pile will accompany your CV if it doesn't lay out its storyline accessibly and, above all, quickly.

Ironically, given that being concise is imperative in terms of the CV you actually send out, the starting point for reinventing your CV is to completely forget about brevity and relevance for now.

GO COMPREHENSIVE

The first task in the building of a new and better CV is to create a full and comprehensive document listing all the roles you've ever held, the dates you were in those roles, your key responsibilities and – most critically – details of your personal achievements in each of those roles. You'll also want to include a comprehensive record of training courses attended and qualifications gained. Also, for each employer you've worked for, put together a two- or three-line statement describing the company in terms of its main activity, size, turnover, number of people employed, etc.

If you're being really thorough about this, you might well find that this document – sometimes called the Director's Cut – runs to six pages or more. That doesn't matter at this stage though. The important point is that you're creating a complete record of your career to date. If you think you've missed something, you might try calling up current and past work colleagues – with varying degrees of discretion – to see whether they remember things you've forgotten.

Armed with this document, you can now start thinking about assembling as many variations of your CV as you need. The point is, you're now perfectly placed to 'pick and mix' the elements from your experience and knowledge that you believe will play best with the person who will read your CV.

Got all you need to start putting a CV together? Have a look at IDEA 6, *What's your type?*, which will help you decide on the format to go for.

Try another idea...

'The only place where success comes before work is in the dictionary.'
VIDAL SASSOON

Defining idea...

How did
it go?

**Q   I simply want to get a good CV together. I wasn't expecting the
Spanish Inquisition to go through my career with a fine
toothcomb. Is it necessary to go into so much detail?**

A   *Most of us lead incredibly busy work lives and so it's easy for important
parts of it to drop off our mental radar. Once you've pulled together as
much information as you can recall about your career, however, there
should be no need to do it again as long as you keep updating.*

**Q   Would it really be so bad if I simply dug out my last CV, tagged on
a few bits and pieces to bring it up to date and then used that as
my calling card?**

A   *That might work sometimes, but don't forget that the job market has
become much more professionalised over the past five to ten years. This
means that when recruiters are shortlisting, adequate CVs will consistently
lose out to their more tailored and polished counterparts. Remember that
your CV will be up against CVs that have been crafted by your competitors
as one-off marketing documents. Can you honestly say that a simple update
of your old CV will stack up against that level of competition?*

3

How long do I have?

The two-page CV has become the Microsoft Windows of job-hunting. It's not about it being the best format, it's just the one that everybody uses. So, just how important is size?

'As far as I'm concerned,' an old recruitment chum told me recently, 'fitting your CV onto two pages is a principle not a rule... but it's a very good principle.'

The Chartered Institute of Personnel and Development, who you'd think ought to know whether or not size matters, offers the following guidance on their website: 'Ideally it should be two pages long with each page printed on a separate sheet.'

Employment agency Manpower gives similar advice, suggesting that: 'Two pages is an ideal length for a CV.'

Outplacement experts RightCoutts take a slightly more relaxed view, advising us to: 'Consider a one-page résumé-style CV or a two- or three-page CV.'

Jobsite, the self-proclaimed 'original, award-winning UK job search and jobs by email service', goes into a bit more detail for visitors to its site: 'The ideal length is two to three pages and one page for the covering letter. If you have just left college

Experiment with form. Produce a one-page version of your CV to supplement your two-pager and then allow yourself the luxury of three pages. Which of the three versions has the most impact? Show them to people whose opinion you value and go with the consensus regardless of length.

you will have less to say but don't pad your CV out with waffle. One page of useful information is undoubtedly worth far more than two pages of irrelevant facts.'

Another employment agency is more succinct and dogmatic: 'Your CV should be no longer than two sides in length.'

From visiting the above websites and a number of others, there seems to be a broad consensus that a two-page CV is probably the safest and most widely accepted length to go for. Life is rarely straightforward and unambiguous, however. Unicom Systems, a long-established IT technical consultancy company, throws that cosy consensus into disarray by dispensing the following advice: 'Often CV guides nominate two pages as the magic length for a CV. Unless you have very little experience, that may be a little light on detail for IT industry requirements. For our purposes, ideal CV length would be three to five (and not more than six) pages, depending on your experience.'

So, IT specialists seem to have a dispensation to go beyond the usual two pages. In fact, this also applies to a wide range of technical roles, including the more big-hitting engineering jobs, where the need for substance and detail outweighs the appeal of brevity. Executives that are more senior also get a bit more leeway, judging from the advice proffered on various senior management recruitment sites. However, unless you fall into one of these categories, the

Defining idea...

'A three-page CV is simply a two-page CV that hasn't been edited tightly enough.'
RICHARD GILBERT, recruitment consultant

odds are heavily in favour of the two-page CV...in principle anyway!

OK, that's enough of this shilly-shallying about the number of pages in the perfect CV. The fact is, you can both bore a recruiter rigid in two pages and keep their interest over three pages, depending on the quality of your content. Here are five unambiguous tips that will improve the quality and impact of your CV:

To get an insight into putting together a CV by US rules, check out IDEA 32, *Transatlantic issues.*

Try another idea...

1. Only include details that positively sell you. Your CV is a marketing document, not a confession.

2. When it comes to describing your knowledge and experience, don't put in information simply because you feel it ought to go in. Keep asking yourself the question, 'Does this fact make it more likely that I'll be called for interview?' If it does, then in it goes.

3. Remember that you want your CV to be read and responded to. Include just enough information to stimulate interest, but not so much that you bore the reader.

4. Make sure the content is relevant to the job you're looking for now, not the one you're looking to leave.

   'If size did matter, the dinosaurs would still be alive.'
   WENDELIN WIEDEKING, Novartis AG Director

   Defining idea...

5. Be brief. Go for short sentences. Steer clear of flowery, descriptive language. A CV is more text message than novel!

How did it go?

Q **My CV comes in at two and a half pages. Why shouldn't I send it out as it is?**

A *There's no rational reason why two and a half pages shouldn't be regarded as perfectly acceptable by recruiters. Given that they all accept two-page CVs without hesitation and three-page CVs with relatively few quibbles, why should something that splits the difference be regarded with such disdain? I don't exaggerate. I've been around recruiters when an odd-length CV turns up and it's as though they've personally experienced an affront to the nature of things.*

So, although there's no sensible reason to adjust the length of your CV, in its current form it would be perceived as an unacceptable breach of CV etiquette by many recruiters and the prospect of you being invited to interview would be slim to non-existent.

Q **So, should I shrink it to two pages or extend it to three?**

A *On the assumption that every word serves a purpose and that there's no additional information you wish to include, I'd be inclined to experiment with presentation. Give the text a bit more air, maybe expand the font, play with a bit more white space and see if a three-pager looks right. On the other hand, as the two-page CV is by far the most popular format in Résumé town, editing it down to two pages might well be the better solution.*

4
Eight potentially life-changing seconds

On average, it takes eight seconds to decide whether to continue reading a CV or to bin it. Here's how to capture and keep the reader's attention in those first vital moments.

At the risk of upsetting 'Fahrenheit 9/11' director Michael Moore, I'd like to propose that anybody about to write their CV should give a tip of their hat to Tony Blair and George Bush.

In recent times, prime ministers and presidents have placed great emphasis on the impact they can make during their first 100 days in office. It's a period of heightened interest for the media and the voters, and a good strong launch can create a positive impetus for the remainder of their term of office. The same principles apply when you're putting together your CV. So, how do you go about grabbing and holding the reader's attention in those first eight seconds?

'Time is money.'
BENJAMIN FRANKLIN

Defining idea...

15

Read your profile statement out loud to yourself. Is the language as natural as possible? There's a tendency for profile statements to be jam-packed with managerial gobbledegook and clichés. So, no 'proactive self-starter' nonsense if you please. That said, you do want to be upbeat and positive about yourself.

The fact is, if you can't convince the reader that you're well worth an interview by the time they're midway down page one of your CV, it's unlikely they'll read much further. Think of the first half of page one as your prime selling space. Your aim should be to try to feature all of your major arguments for being interviewed in that space.

Writing a CV isn't like writing a novel where you slowly tease and intrigue the reader, building gradually to a compelling climax. With a CV, your impact must be front-end loaded. There's no point in introducing a new and compelling piece of information halfway down the second page of your CV, as chances are the reader won't reach that point and so it won't be noticed.

So, what's the best information to put on that first half page? Well, virtually all recruiters expect to see your name and contact details at the top of the first page. Not just your name, address and home telephone number, by the way. You should also include your mobile number and an email address, as these are good indicators of your technological literacy.

Defining
idea...

'When I've got say 50 or 60 CVs to look through, I simply don't have time to go through them all in detail.'
JOHN VILLIS, recruitment manager

After your contact details, I'd recommend including a two- or three-line profile statement. We'll go into more detail about profiles elsewhere, but for now think of it as a sixty- to eighty-word précis of what you have to offer that would make you a prime contender for the position you're going for.

The profile statement is the single most important element of the first page of your CV, so check out IDEA 5, *Me in a nutshell*, for some pointers.

Try another idea...

By the time you've included contact details and a profile statement, you should still have around a half to two-thirds of that first half page still available to you. What follows the profile will vary according to what elements of your background and experience most closely match what the recruiter is looking for. If they're trying to recruit somebody who can do A, B and C, then you'll need to show explicit evidence of your attainments and experience at doing A, B and C. If this evidence can best be shown in your current/most recent role, then you'll probably want to go straight into your career history. If, on the other hand, you need to draw on your broader career and experience to prove your competence at A, B and C, a section called something like Key Achievements or Key Skills & Experience would suit your purpose better.

The recruiter is only likely to read on beyond this first portion of your CV if they're convinced you explicitly meet the specification they're recruiting against. This is therefore not the time for subtlety. Above all, don't rely on the recruiter to draw inferences from the information you provide. Concentrate on filling that first half page with as much relevant information as you can, paying particular attention to addressing the job and person requirements that the recruiter has stated. Given this, it goes without saying that to feature a piece of information that the recruiter is likely to regard as irrelevant is a definite no-no.

'Time is precious, but truth is more precious than time.'
BENJAMIN DISRAELI

Defining idea...

17

How did it go?

Q   Is eight seconds for real? I didn't realise recruiters were quite that lazy!

A   *Pretty much. Some studies suggest that the figure could be as low as three seconds, but no more than thirty seconds max on average. It's pragmatism as opposed to laziness in my view. Do the sums. A typical advertisement in the Sunday papers pulls in around 500 applications. Realistically, if there's one post to fill, then eight to ten interviewees should do the trick, with maybe half a dozen candidates in reserve. The recruiter's challenge is therefore to whittle the applications down from 500 to fifteen as quickly and fairly as possible. Allowing two minutes per CV would mean over two days spent going through them all. Besides, when they're in a position to eliminate 97% of the applicants, they can set high standards for making the shortlist. They can also afford to reject candidates for relatively minor reasons.*

Q   When companies are shortlisting on that basis, how can they be sure they're getting the best candidates?

A   *They can't. The process is designed to pick up those people who convey succinctly and explicitly how they meet the selection criteria. The candidate who might be the best in reality yet doesn't convey their proposition effectively is always in danger of missing out.*

5
Me in a nutshell

Present employers with a profile statement that sums up your proposition concisely.

At their best, profile statements are like a good advertisement — snappy, focused and enticing. At their worst, they reek of tired management speak and self-congratulatory bullshit.

A profile statement (sometimes called a summary statement) is your opportunity to distil down what you have to offer a potential employer to a few well-chosen words (typically around three or four lines' worth). It appears on the first page of the CV, most commonly straight after the name and contact details, and should give a concise overview of your relevant skills, experience and qualifications.

Your profile statement is your first real opportunity to grab the reader's attention. Its importance should not be underestimated. We talked earlier about how somebody reading your CV decides whether or not you're worth an interview within an average of just eight seconds. By the time they've read your profile, a

Don't try to produce your profile statement until you've written the first draft of your CV. It's supposed to convey the essence of your CV in a few short lines, so at least have to hand a rough outline of all the points you wish to cover in your CV.

significant number of recruiters will already have decided whether or not you might fit the bill. Get the tone and content of the profile wrong and you're heading for the reject pile. Catch the recruiter's eye in a positive way and at least you can count on the next few lines of your CV being looked at.

The profile generally has three elements to it:

1. Function, level, sector

2. Key strengths in regard to the vacancy applied for

3. Accountability or contribution

FUNCTION, LEVEL, SECTOR

This reflects the type of job you do, the level you do it at and the sector(s) where you have gained your experience. For example, you might be one of the following:

- Qualified Accountant operating at senior management level in the manufacturing sector.

- Experienced and resourceful General Manager with proven background in the packing industry.

- Part-qualified HR professional with a strong recruitment background gained in the financial sector.

Once you've got your profile statement together, think about your elevator pitch. More about that in IDEA 44, *Perfect your personal elevator pitch.*

Try another idea...

You'll notice in the second and third examples that the basic information is supplemented by adjectives, which are there to add more detail about the individual. This is a good tactic, but don't waste your time including adjectives that are weak or neutral. Examples of positive personal characteristics include: results-orientated, energetic, creative, adaptable, articulate, logical, committed and leading edge.

The other thing to notice about all three examples is that they all describe the applicant in the third person, which is very much the norm in profile statements and what I would always recommend. The curious thing about writing a profile statement is that it's you writing nice, positive words about, well, you. It's only a literary conceit I guess, but the use of the third person does play that down a shade.

KEY STRENGTHS IN REGARD TO THE VACANCY APPLIED FOR

'In regard to the vacancy' is a key phrase. This is not the moment to set out the all-singing, all-dancing, wide-screen picture of absolutely everything you're good at. If the recruiting organisation is looking for somebody who is strong at A, B and C, then you need to focus on your personal capabilities at doing A, B and C. An example of this element of the profile would be: 'Highly experienced sales negotiator, with strong project and cost management skills.'

'Few have strength of reason to overrule the perceptions of sense, and yet fewer have curiosity or benevolence to struggle long against the first impression: he who therefore fails to please in his salutation and address is at once rejected, and never obtains an opportunity of showing his latest excellences or essential qualities.'
SAMUEL JOHNSON

ACCOUNTABILITY OR CONTRIBUTION

This is your opportunity to indicate what you contribute to an organisation's performance. Here are some examples:

- Proven track record of successfully managing IT projects in excess of 10 million.

- Successfully turned around three loss-making businesses, bringing each into profit within two years of arrival.

- Internal consultant with a strong background in change management.

WORD OF WARNING: WHERE'S THE BEEF?

By putting together each of these three elements, you can create a strong, incisive profile. Remember though that whilst you're at liberty to describe yourself in very complimentary terms, you'll need to provide 'proof' of your accomplishments elsewhere in your CV. As a Recruitment Consultant once told me: 'Profiles are basically bullshit unless there's real concrete evidence to back them up.'

Q   I've had a few cracks at writing my profile statement, but I'm still not happy with the results. Any tips?

How did it go?

A   *If you've followed the three-point structure I've suggested and put everything into the third person, you won't have gone too far wrong. Often the problem we have with our profiles is that we're just not used to describing ourselves in positive, achievement-orientated terms. Because of this, we can slip into using a curious mix of management speak and clichés. And before we know it, there's a whiff of cheese! To avoid this, try to express yourself in your own natural vocabulary. It is possible to put together a plain-speaking profile that impresses recruiters without the need for a sick bucket!*

Q   I've had another go at writing my profile, but now it seems a bit, well, dull. What do you suggest?

A   *The important thing about a profile is that it conveys to the recruiter the sort of person they're looking for. If they're after someone who's creative and innovative with lots of flair, then the language of the profile needs be quite exuberant in response. If, on the other hand, they're looking for a solid, reliable, experienced person, then they're likely to find exuberant language off-putting.*

23

6

What's your type?

The two main types of CV in circulation are the reverse chronological and the functional. They can both work extremely well, but which to use when?

One of the more important decisions to make concerning your CV is how to structure the information you want to present. There are many variations on a theme, but the decision really boils down to one of two options.

Let's have a quick look at each in turn:

THE REVERSE CHRONOLOGICAL CV

This type of CV details your education and the jobs you've held in sequence. The most effective use of a chronological CV is to list your experience in reverse order, i.e. starting with your current or most recent role and then moving back in time, and then treating your education in the same way.

Here's an idea for you... **Produce your CV in a different format to the one you normally use, and compare the two. You might surprise yourself with how good the alternative version looks. Then consider experimenting with a format that mixes both styles.**

The standard layout would be as follows:

Part One	Contact details (name, address, telephone numbers, email)
Part Two	Profile statement
Part Three	Career history (providing the most detail about your most recent role, with previous roles taking up progressively less space)
Part Four	Education and training/professional qualifications (also in reverse chronological order, so that you're emphasising your most recent attainments)
Part Five	Interests (try to give examples that suggest a good mixture of positive qualities like leadership, personal fitness, intellectual capability, etc.)
Part Six	Personal information (age, marital status, children, etc.). This information is optional, although recruiters seem to prefer to have these details.

The main benefit of a chronological layout is that the first page of your CV features prominently your most recent (and typically most senior) role. Remember, you only have seconds to grab the attention of the person reading your CV, so you want to make sure that you get all your big-hitting points across early.

There are some drawbacks to the chronological CV, however, notably that:

- If you're a bit of a job-hopper, this type of CV will display that very graphically.
- Any gaps in your career history are likely to stand out.
- Your skills and achievements may not be signalled clearly to the reader if they're spread over a number of the roles you've held.
- If your most recent role is a different type of role to the one you've applied for, this may instil doubt into the mind of the reader.

That said, the chronological CV is still by far the most widely used format. In fact, it's reckoned that around 80–90% of CVs in circulation follow the chronological format. Moreover, the vast majority of recruitment managers prefer to see a candidate's information in this format.

Gain a deeper insight into writing up your achievements by motoring along to IDEA 23, *Take the CAR*, which looks at structure and presentation of your career triumphs.

Try another idea...

'*It is not enough to do your best; you must know what to do, and then do your best.*'
W. EDWARDS DEMING

Defining idea...

THE FUNCTIONAL CV

This type of CV is organised by skill rather than job title. It pays no heed to chronology and instead focuses on the individual's skills and abilities that are relevant to the role applied for. Examples of areas that might be relevant are leadership, project management, customer service and so on.

The functional CV can be productive if your most recent career history isn't particularly indicative of future direction. The main drawbacks are that it's more time-consuming to draw up and that people more used to seeing 'traditional' chronological CVs sometimes regard it with a degree of suspicion.

EMPHASISE YOUR ACHIEVEMENTS

Whichever format you decide to go with, make sure you concentrate on what you've achieved in your various roles and where you've made a positive difference. Don't simply produce a series of potted job descriptions. The focus should be less on the nitty-gritty of your job responsibilities and more on your personal impact.

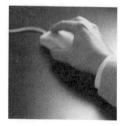 

Q   **I'm still struggling to understand when to use a chronological or a functional CV. Can you help?**

How did it go?

A   *The chronological CV draws the recruiter's attention to your recent job history and experience. It therefore works particularly well when you're looking to continue in the same type of role and industry. It also enables you to highlight a steady progression in your field. For the more traditional employers, it's the format they're most familiar and comfortable with. The functional CV draws attention to the skills and strengths you've amassed over the course of your career. It works well when you want to make a significant career change because it puts the emphasis on your transferable skills. If you've been with one employer for a long time, it can usefully shift attention towards all the skills you've acquired in the role and averts it away from your single employer. On the other side of the coin, focusing on skills and experience can take the edge off a history of frequent job-hopping.*

Q   **Which type of CV is currently in fashion?**

A   *The best CV to use will vary according to circumstances, but a chronological CV that also gives some examples of achievements in each role will take some beating. It's also important to remember that the chronological and functional formats are only two basic templates. There's no reason why you shouldn't create a hybrid of the two if you feel it gets your proposition over more compellingly.*

7

D.I.Y.C.V.

The title may well remind you of a certain catchy song from the 1970s, but D.I.Y.C.V. actually has a very contemporary message.

Whilst browsing the classifieds have you noticed the growing legion of companies who will put together a state-of-the-art CV on your behalf for a sizeable wad of cash?

On the face of it, you might think this is an attractive offer. After all, very few of us are professional writers (I suspect my editor will be nodding meaningfully at this point). And even those of us with a decent turn of phrase might not be au fait with what's in and out of fashion in the world of CVs. You might therefore think there's some sense in handing responsibility over to a professional CV writer who is familiar with the latest tricks and techniques and who can ensure that your CV looks contemporary and is jam-packed with the latest jargon and buzz phrases.

Tempting though these services might seem, I'd keep my money in my pocket if I were you and use it for something else. Here are four reasons why it's important for you to write your CV yourself:

Here's an idea for you... **Go and look at some other CVs, and feel free to swipe ideas creatively from other sources in terms of the layout, structure and wording of your CV – CV writing isn't like taking an exam where to look over somebody's shoulder is to cheat. You should be able to track down a good number of sample CVs from the internet.**

1. A professional CV writer won't necessarily understand the terminology specific to your particular line of work and therefore there's a danger that they might misrepresent your experience.

2. Getting somebody else to write your CV will still require a decent amount of effort on your part. Typically, you'll still need to provide a written outline of your career to date and spend some time talking through your career history.

3. CVs produced by third parties can all too often read like a production line job, rather than the product of your own efforts. I have an HR chum who swears that she can spot not only whether somebody has had help with putting their CV together but also in many cases which particular company or agency provided the assistance.

4. Most critically, imagine securing an interview using a CV that was written by somebody else. There you are sat opposite an interviewer who has those two sides of A4 on the table in front of them. How confident are you that you could respond positively and confidently to an interviewer who could pick up on any

phrase in the CV and probe you about it? All of a sudden, that rather natty piece of management speak which you never fully understood in the first place can come back to haunt you. A confident interview

Assuming you're happy to craft your own CV, turn back to IDEA 2, *Remember, remember*, for some pointers.

Try another idea...

performance depends on you feeling comfortable talking through your CV and so it's vital for you to understand it in depth. In this case, depth of understanding comes from being the creator of the CV not the commissioner.

These reasons aside, remember that a CV is a one-to-one marketing document. Are you prepared to have your CV professionally redrafted ever time you want to apply for a job? Moreover, could you afford it?

Look, I don't want to suggest that there's absolutely no value in these CV-writing services. There may be some merit in getting a first draft of your CV produced by a professional agency, particularly if you're prone to suffer from CV writer's block or if you just don't find it easy to express yourself in writing. However, you must bear in mind that you'll still need to tweak – or perhaps even substantially change – the CV every time it goes out to make sure that you emphasise the key attributes you have relative to the position you're going after.

'Imitation is suicide.'
RALPH WALDO EMERSON

Defining idea...

How did it go?

Q **I took on board your caveats about CV-writing services, but decided to splash out on one regardless. I think it looks pretty good, so is there any reason why I shouldn't use it?**

A *If you genuinely think that it will sell you better than compiling your own CV would, then it's probably a decent option. The killer question is whether it genuinely represents the best way to put your CV in circulation. Bear in mind that each job you apply for might be looking for subtly or maybe even wildly different qualities. Does your bought CV pick up on these distinctions? If not, how easy is it to adapt? Did you get a copy of the CV on disk so that you can refashion it if you choose to or did you simply receive a set number of copies?*

Q **Is there anything else I need to watch out for?**

A *Make sure you continue to cast an eye back over your knowledge and experience each time you decide to apply for something. I don't want to sound trite, but the people who drafted your CV only know what you told them. How confident are you that you've supplied them with all the relevant information? Sure you've not forgotten anything?*

8

Cut to the chase

Score points with the reader for every line of your CV and concentrate on identifying your high value content.

Your CV shouldn't be an unexpurgated account of your life to date. Recruiters simply won't be interested in the likes of that cycling proficiency badge you gained at the age of ten.

When a recruiter tells you that your CV is 'comprehensive', it's not always a compliment. The better your CV is edited and the more it focuses on the particular needs of the job you're going for, the better your chances of getting an interview.

Here are a few tips on how to play the various sections of your CV:

EXPERIENCE

When you provide details of the jobs you've held, the main areas you need to focus on for each role are:

■ Your position, the organisation where you work(ed) and the relevant dates

Here's an idea for you... **Try this test on the first draft of your CV. Highlight in green the lines you think positively sell you against the specific vacancy you're applying for. Use yellow to highlight any 'neutral' information that neither sells nor harms you. And then red for anything that the recruiter might consider negative or problematic. What does the balance of shadings tell you?**

- An outline of responsibilities and accountabilities

- Your personal and managerial skills

- Any significant achievements

Once you've compiled all this information, you should ask yourself three key questions:

1. Is this information relevant to the needs of the reader?

2. Does it provide positive evidence of my skills and competence?

3. Does this information add value?

EDUCATION AND QUALIFICATIONS

Don't automatically trot out every single qualification you hold. Judge how much detail the reader is likely to be interested in, given the job you're going for. For example, if you're applying to be Director of Finance in a blue-chip company, chances are that the grade you got in your woodworking exam twenty years ago isn't going to be one of your most impressive trump cards. On the other hand, it would be extremely relevant if you want to be considered for a carpentry apprenticeship.

PERSONAL INFORMATION

There's an argument for including date of birth, marital status (although recruiters tell me this isn't necessary most of the time) and possibly whether you hold a full driving licence. Just about everything else is unnecessarily self-revealing. You certainly don't need to give details of the number of children you have and their ages (and definitely not their names).

If you're struggling to keep the length of your CV down, have a look at IDEA 3, *How long do I have?*

Try another idea...

GENERAL

Eliminate unnecessary headings

For example, there's no need to put 'Curriculum Vitae' at the top of your CV. Besides stating the obvious, it takes up valuable space that you could devote to making a selling point.

Keep it short

As far as possible, stick to two sides of A4. CVs are subject to the whims of changing taste, but just now long and detailed CVs are definitely out of fashion. Besides, keeping it short forces you to be concise and relevant.

Use active verbs

Just compare the punch of active verbs like 'implemented', 'launched' and 'optimised' with the rather more mundane 'maintained', 'administered', 'recorded' and even 'managed'. Active verbs will give your CV more zip and impact.

'He knew the precise psychological moment when to say nothing.'
OSCAR WILDE, *The Picture of Dorian Gray*

Defining idea...

37

Stuff to leave out

As a rule, don't include:

- The reason(s) why you're leaving your current job

- The salary you're looking for

- References

- Political allegiances

- Pre-senior school education

- The months when you changed/started jobs (just the years will do)

- A photograph

There's an acid test to apply when deciding what to put in and what to leave out. Go through your CV and ask yourself whether each piece of information makes it more likely that you'll be invited to interview. Some pieces of information are neutral but necessary, such as your name and contact details, but the vast majority of the content should be positive and relevant.

Q   **I've had a go at that three-colour exercise you suggested and I have a balance of around 50% green, 40% yellow and 10% red. Now what do I do?**

How did it go?

A   *Here's a clue. Unless your first page is predominantly green following your contact details, you're unlikely to get shortlisted.*

Q   **OK, got that. Anything else?**

A   *Well, the best CVs I've seen have a mix of around 80% green, 20% yellow and 0% red. The first issue you need to address is that red percentage. Given that this is your marketing document, to have 10% of your CV going against you is bad news. Actually, it's disastrous news if there's anything highlighted in red on page one of your CV. So, first delete all the red bits. Next, look at the amount of yellow material you have in your CV. The only yellow bits you should have are your contact details (your location may be a green factor, but let's not get too picky), maybe some elements of your personal details, possibly some stages of your early career and lastly any qualifications and training that might not connect directly to the job you're going for. Decide what proportion of that yellow stuff is vital and delete the rest. Chances are you now have lots more valuable space open for green business, so build in some more achievements for starters.*

9

Throw another log on the file

Devise a good tracking system – vital for when you've a number of job search activities on the go.

If you've ever wandered around a supermarket desperately trying to remember what you were there to buy, you have my sympathy and kinship.

Perhaps I'm unusual in having grey cells that simply don't jump to attention the way they used to, but I suspect that in these multitasking, information-overloaded, nanosecond noughties, we're all a bit prone to losing track of the odd strand of the plot. This can be particularly true when we're looking to change jobs, as there's a lot of fiddly detail we need to keep tabs on. Here are some possible examples:

- How many job applications do I have on the go?
- How long is it since I requested that application form?
- Which version of my CV did I send to company X?
- How's the ratio of CVs sent out to interviews gained?
- When am I supposed to ring that networking contact again?

Here's an idea for you... **Make sure you have ready access to any necessary records. If admin is your worst nightmare, however, you may prefer to simply keep all the relevant information in your head or jot the odd note in your diary.**

If you agree that a tracking system might be useful, I'd recommend up to four different logs, namely:

- A job-search log
- A weekly activity log
- A networking log
- A career log

The first two are relevant only when you're actively job searching. The final two underpin a broader, more long-term approach to career management. A definition of what each log is designed to do follows, as well as a series of headings to indicate the kind of information you might want to record. These headings aren't meant to be prescriptive; feel free to add or subtract headings to your heart's content.

JOB-SEARCH LOG

Purpose
To enable you to keep an accurate record of all the job applications you have on the go.

Possible headings
- Vacancy.
- Source of vacancy (e.g. press ad, job centre, tip-off, agency).
- Where the vacancy was advertised (if applicable).
- Date of advert (if applicable).
- Date and nature of first contact (e.g. job information pack requested, telephone conversation with agency).
- Date CV submitted.

- Version of CV submitted. (It's crucial to keep tabs on this. If you go along to an interview you'll want to know what information you've already given them. It will also reflect whether one version of your CV is generating a particularly good response.)
- Date of interview.
- Date of second interview.
- Follow-up phone calls.
- Outcome of application.

Turn to IDEA 43, *Networking*, for some pointers on building your contacts list.

Try another idea...

WEEKLY ACTIVITY LOG

Purpose
To enable you to plan intended job-search activity over the coming seven days.

Possible headings
- People to contact.
- Approach letters to send.
- Thank you letters and follow-ups.
- Planned networking activity.
- Topics to research.
- Ads to respond to.

'When I try to remember, I always forget.'
WINNIE THE POOH

Defining idea...

NETWORKING LOG

Purpose
To enable you to keep an accurate record of all the contacts you have made.

Possible headings

- Name of contact.
- Job title.
- Organisation.
- Address.
- Phone.
- Email.
- Date of meeting.
- Length of meeting.
- Record of what came out of meeting.
- Referred by (i.e. who introduced you to this networking contact).

CAREER LOG

Purpose

To keep yourself market-ready by keeping an ongoing record of material that might feed into your next CV.

Possible headings

You might want to add an entry into this log each time you complete a major project, achieve something notable, acquire a significant new skill or expand your area of knowledge or experience. Details to include are:

- A relevant date
- Any change in your current job title, reporting relationships or scope of responsibilities
- The situation or challenge you faced
- The actions you took
- The results (quantified if possible) you achieved

Q **I'm not averse to a bit of record keeping, but isn't keeping all these logs excessive?**

How did
it go?

A *If it seems excessive, it probably is excessive, for you at least. The logs shouldn't simply while away a few hours a week, they need to be active management tools or they have little value. The two that are of particular value if you're job-hunting are the job-search log and the networking log. The weekly activity log and career log are short-term and long-term planning tools respectively.*

Q **Two down, two to go! But the job-search log and the networking log still seem a bit heavy-handed to me. Do I really need to keep them?**

A *Perhaps you're only conducting a low-key job search. If you can hold all the relevant information in your head, I'd suggest that the emphasis should shift from the logs to increasing your general level of activity! Certainly, once you start networking to any productive level, you should find it helpful to have a record of events. And if your primary contacts are happy to introduce you to people they know (i.e. your secondary contacts), who in turn set up further contacts, then you can rapidly become confused.*

10

Learn to speak 'behaviourese'

Use your CV as a tool to illustrate your competencies and you'll really impress the recruiters.

Over 70% of UK organisations now have competency systems in place, sometimes covering just the key roles in the organisation but often embracing every job.

Broadly speaking, competencies are skills or characteristic actions used by individuals to enable them to cope successfully with a variety of situations both within and outside of work. In a nutshell, they define the skills and behaviours that are directly related to superior performance in a given role.

Alongside all the organisations that have competency systems, most professions have come up with their own set of competency standards. And not just the obvious professions like personnel, accountancy, etc. In 1999, for example, the British Standards Institution published a professional standard for nightclub bouncers.

Here's an idea for you... **Keep a behavioural log in which you can record behavioural evidence on a regular basis. This will put you in pole position when you come to update your CV or fill in an application form in the future.**

Although the headings change from company to company and from profession to profession, the following are some of the most commonly found competency elements:

Achievement drive

Analytical thinking

Business integrity

Business knowledge

Change orientation

Communicating and influencing

Contribution to results

Creative thinking

Customer focus

Decision-making

Facilitation

Financial management

Handling information

Innovation

Interpersonal sensitivity

Judgement

Leadership

Networking

Openness to ideas

People development

Planning and organisation

Preference for action

Problem solving

Professionalism

Self-confidence

Strategic thinking

Teamwork

Technical knowledge

Tenacity

Thinking skills

If you work or have worked in an environment that uses a competency system, you'll know that they're regularly used to support recruitment and performance monitoring, as well as training and development activity.

These days most job advertisements explicitly identify the competencies that the successful candidate will need to have. Just to take a couple of examples from the appointments section of a weekend paper, one advertisement for a Managing Director refers to the need for, amongst other things, a high level of skill in the following: team building, change management, results orientation and a 'hands on' mentality. Another job calls for someone with integrity, robustness, analytical skills and a gift for leadership.

Anybody wishing to apply for either of those jobs would need to be able to demonstrate a proven capability in these competency areas. A Personal Qualities section in your CV that simply mirrors these skill areas isn't enough. To say that you have highly developed team-building skills, for example, doesn't mean that recruiters will automatically swoon at the very thought of you coming along to interview. No, they will expect to see a piece of evidence to back up your assertion. If you can show specifically how you demonstrated team-building qualities, then you might be in with a sniff. Perhaps you might go for something along the following lines:

If you're not convinced you've got the best possible examples, check out IDEA 41, I'll show you mine if you show me yours, which discusses the merits of getting a second opinion.

Try another idea...

'It ain't what you do it's the way that you do it. That's what gets results.'
As sung by ELLA FITZGERALD, BANANARAMA, BIG BROVAZ and many more besides

Defining idea...

Instigated a series of 'Working in Harmony' workshops at a time when cross team working was virtually non-existent and morale generally low. Won the company's Team of the Year award, and the latest employee survey revealed a significant hike in morale levels.

With application forms, the challenge to provide evidence of various competencies is often made explicitly. Forms are often designed to include a series of headings like Decision Making, Leadership and Problem Solving. The applicant then has to give concrete examples of a time when they had to display effective decision-making skills, and so on.

Giving examples can be more difficult than you might imagine. How easy would you find it, say, to come up with an account of a time when you had to display a high level of integrity? It's not how most of us naturally file our organisational experience. Instead, we move from task to task, rarely pausing long enough to capture behavioural evidence from our work life. This becomes a real problem when we want to change jobs and we're asked to come up with lots of evidence and examples.

Q **Good grief! Has the world gone mad? Competency systems seem like a new cottage industry for the HR department to me.**

How did it go?

A *That's not really true. Competency-based selection methods have actually been shown to be about the fairest recruitment system around. A competency-based approach is only concerned with what people actually do in their jobs; it's not bothered about job titles and it takes no note of how we might respond to hypothetical situations. Imagine you're in an interview and somebody asks you how you'd react in a crisis. In that hypothetical world, I'm sure that we'd all stay calm and show any necessary leadership traits. In the real world of competencies, the question would be along the lines of, 'Tell me about a time when you've had to deal with a crisis situation.' In response, we'd have to describe how we have actually behaved.*

Q **Enough! This is beginning to sound like a Competency Party broadcast. I'm not sure how to use competencies in my CV, so can you concentrate on that please?**

A *As I mentioned earlier, competencies are skills or characteristic actions we use to deal with situations in and outside of work. So, when you describe specifically how you did something, you're using competency language. This shows up in CVs in the form of action statements, i.e. what we actually did to achieve certain results. If you want to develop your fluency in 'behaviourese', have a look at the list of competencies above and see if you can come up with an example of a time when you needed to demonstrate each of those traits. Make a note of what you personally did and you have the makings of your own personal database.*

51

11

Reading the runes

How to interpret job advertisements and ensure your CV reflects what's required.

OK, so you've scoured the papers, trade magazines and the web and you've come across something you rather like the sound of. Now comes the difficult bit...

HOW TO ANALYSE AN ADVERTISEMENT

In their book *Brilliant CV*, Jim Bright and Joanne Earl offer up a helpful set of questions that might enable you to get to grips with a job advertisement:

1. What don't you understand about the job ad?

2. What type of industry is it in? What's happening in the company or industry? Is it restructuring or expanding?

3. What is the main purpose of the role being offered?

4. Why is this role important to the company? How will this role affect the company's bottom line?

Here's an
idea for
you...

Be explicit about how you meet the specification in your covering letter. If the advertisement asks for somebody who can do A, B and C, then your covering letter should detail how A, B and C are the very things you do best.

5. What type of skills do they want? What other skills might be needed, given the job's purpose?

6. What types of knowledge/training do they want? What other knowledge or training might be needed, given the job's purpose?

MATCHING REQUIREMENTS

Read the advertisement carefully to build up your diagnosis of the sort of person the recruiter is after. Differentiate between the essential requirements and those that are desirable. Most requirements will be explicit, but some may be implicit and require you to read between the lines.

For example, in March 2001 a county council was seeking applicants for a PR post that would involve promoting bus transport, yet a company car was being offered with the job. A representative for the council was quoted as hoping that the person appointed would demonstrate personal commitment to the job by not taking up the car offer. Now there's one way to impress/not impress the council!

Sometimes, what we imagine to be essential is sometimes either desirable or unnecessary. In July 2004, the British press reported with great amusement that the newly appointed chairman of the Melton Mowbray Pork Pie Association, Matthew O'Callaghan, was a vegetarian.

If the ad mentions a website reference, that's your first port of call research-wise. If it doesn't, it's still worth using a search engine to try and track down their website. A company's website will help you to build your understanding of the company and may well provide further information about the vacancy.

For more on covering letters look at IDEA 33, *Please find attached...*

Try another idea...

Ordinarily, you'll need to show that you can meet practically 100% of the essential requirements and around 50–70% of the desirable qualities sought. However, when the labour market is a bit tight and there just aren't that many people job-hunting, you can afford to drop the former to 70–80%. The desirables become almost irrelevant if the recruiter is likely to get a low response to their advertisement.

When you examine the job requirements in detail, you'll find that you match each of the recruiter's requirements at different levels. These can be characterised as:

- High match
- Medium match
- Low or no match

Where you have a high match, make sure that this is glaringly apparent in both your covering letter and CV. Where you have a medium match, include this in the CV but not in any covering letter. If you can only muster a low match or no match, bury this towards the back of the CV or – better still – don't mention it at all!

'Your insight serves you well.'
OBI-WAN KENOBI

Defining idea...

55

How did
it go?

Q I've just seen a job that I'd love to apply for. What should I do next?

A   Start by reading the advertisement very carefully, asking yourself what the organisation is looking for. Most of the requirements will be explicitly set out: experience of this; holding a qualification in that; proven leader/team-builder/decision-maker or whatever. Make a list of these requirements and ask yourself whether you meet them.

Q What if I don't have everything that the advertisement asks for?

A   It's often the case that applicants don't have every qualification or piece of experience mentioned in the advertisement. Try to determine what the 'must-haves' are. These aren't necessarily what the advert describes as essential. For example, 'Must have a good working knowledge of Sage accounting software' might well mean in reality 'If you know a different piece of accounting software, we'd be prepared to pay for some Sage training to bring you up to speed.' Also, 'Must have a degree' often isn't as inflexible as it sounds. As a rough guideline, if you can match 70% of the stated requirements, it can be worth going for. After all, you've nothing to lose but the price of a stamp. Oh and by the way, resist any miserly tendencies and go for first-class post.

12

What am I letting myself in for?

The better you understand your target company, the more targeted you can make your CV. Which is why you'd be wise to find out as much as possible about your next potential employer.

If you uncover a potential corporate 'basket case', then I'd advise against joining them. If a company comes through your research with flying colours, however, then it should make an impressive addition to your CV.

Here are five ways to carry out the research required to separate the Enrons of this world from the pick of the bunch:

1. Phone a friend

Start putting the word around and you may track down somebody (or somebody who knows somebody) who either works for the company or is a customer a supplier of theirs. These informal sources of information can be an invaluable guide to what's really going on inside the company.

Here's an idea for you...

Ask yourself how good a potential employer is compared to where you're currently working. Remember that the company you go on to join will be the company that will take pride of place at the head of your CV the next time you make a move. How do you think that will play with future employers? Will they be impressed?

2. Google them

The amount of information to be found on the internet is quite staggering. In the pre-internet days, it could be quite difficult to research a company. Nowadays, to turn up at an interview without a detailed understanding of the company is almost unforgivable. You don't have to use Google of course. Personally, I'm quite fond of mooter.com.

3. The company website

Most companies of any kind of size will have one. Many of the best sites include an online copy of annual reports, information on company structures, copies of vision or mission statements, press releases and links to related sites. If you don't know the website address, it's always worth trying www.[name of company].com, .co.uk, .fr, .de... Failing that, a decent search engine should get you there pretty quickly. If there isn't a company website, that in itself carries a bit of a message.

Defining idea...

'To be conscious that you are ignorant is a great step to knowledge.'
BENJAMIN DISRAELI

4. Get hold of an annual report

You can often do this online via the company's website. There are also a number of ordering services you can use. In the UK, for example, it's worth using a service like the Financial Times' Annual Reports service, operated by WIL-Link (go to www.worldinvestorlink.com

where you can ask for any number of reports to be sent to your address free of charge). Alternatively, phone the companies direct and ask them to send you a copy.

5. Track newspapers and journals

Scan the newspapers if you can, particularly the broadsheets and business journals like *The Economist*. If something is in the papers, chances are that the topic may well be high in the minds of people who work there.

You should be able to directly incorporate some of the information you uncover into your CV or covering letter. In fact, this should be a specific aim of yours, as there's real added value in letting the company know that you've put time and effort into finding out about them. And, of course, should you be invited to interview, you'll already have done a lot of the legwork to prepare yourself for that part of the selection process.

One final point. Leaving one job for another is a significant life decision. An informed decision is always likely to yield a better outcome than a leap into the dark. Before you think of resigning, are you confident that you know enough about the new role and the new company, such as its culture, the state of the balance sheet, and so on?

If you're on the point of joining another organisation, consider looking back at IDEA 1, *Dream a little dream*, to make sure you're still on track to achieve your career goals.

Try another idea...

'I know all the tourist things. I know about the Queen, Buckingham Palace, driving on the left-hand side of the road and fish and chips.'
MALACHI DAVIS, American athlete, insisting he had the right credentials to represent Great Britain at the 2004 Olympics (and did)

Defining idea...

59

How did
it go?

Q **I've uncovered one or two bits of information about a company I'm interested in that I'm not sure I like the look of. What do I do now?**

A *This will depend on precisely what's concerning you. I'd suggest that you don't give even weight to every piece of information you dig up. If you've managed to have a chat with somebody working inside the company and you're happy that they have given you a balanced view, then that probably deserves a greater weighting than some newspaper sources. If you've popped the company name into Google and have come across a website that features a rant by an ex-employee, be more sanguine. By and large, I recommend giving the company the benefit of the doubt. After all, if you don't apply for a job on the back of your research, you may never know find out whether that research was unfair. You can always withdraw your application at a later stage.*

Q **I've come across a job I'd like to go for with a small start-up company, but unfortunately I'm really struggling to get any information at all about these people. How can I get the facts I need to make a decision?**

A *It's a fact of business life that some companies will have no track record to speak of, but perhaps they have marketing material they can send you or maybe even a business plan. I'd be a bit surprised at the lack of a website, but you may have no choice but to get into conversation with them and then make your judgement in the light of what you been able to discover.*

13

Ditch the dodgy dossier

Resist the temptation to sex up the content of your CV.

According to research reported in 'TIME' magazine, the average person is lied to about 200 times a day. Apparently, men lie roughly 20% more than women do, but women are better at it.

Around 41% of our lies are intended to conceal misbehaviour (e.g. the classic 'Sorry darling, but I need to work late tonight'), while another 20% are those little white lies that make social life manageable (e.g. 'We'd love to come to dinner on Saturday, but unfortunately we've got something else on'). And different national cultures view telling fibs with varying degrees of seriousness; the Japanese are the world's least comfortable fibbers, whereas Russians are the most habitual liars.

Given all the above, if a Russian male tells you that he can't come to dinner because he needs to work, chances are he's fibbing.

Scrutinize your CV and delete any elements that you'd struggle to talk through at an interview. Alternatively, reword them so that you feel more comfortable.

Taking into account this widespread capacity for mendacity, it's not surprising that our tendency to stretch the truth sometimes shows up in our CVs. In fact, it's reckoned that around 25% of CVs contain lies. When the CV-verifying company CV Check approaches candidates to tell them it has been engaged by a potential employer to check applications, up to 20% of the original applicants ask to withdraw from the recruitment process.

The most common type of lie on a CV relates to qualifications. I've seen CVs with school grades inflated, fictitious degrees and trumped-up professional qualifications.

In many cases people own up under the slightest amount of pressure at interview. And it won't surprise you to learn that they're never offered the jobs. It's not so much the exposed lie(s) itself that's the problem, it's more that it undermines the credibility of the rest of the information given in the CV. It may well be that 99% of the CV describes genuine accomplishments, but that errant 1% casts fatal doubt in the mind of the recruiter.

Apart from the habitual liars in our presence, I suspect that most people perform better at an interview when they know that their CV contains 100% bona fide information. The ability to look an interviewer in the eye, secure in the knowledge that a line-by-line scrutiny of your CV will reveal nothing untoward, will boost your confidence no end.

The unequivocal advice here is to be honest when writing your CV. Don't fabricate evidence in your CV or in any way dress up the truth. It might be tempting to make yourself even more irresistible to a potential employer by augmenting reality with a few fictional excesses. Don't do it, however, as the truth is liable to come out at some point, leaving you facing anything from mild embarrassment to rejection by a potential employer or dismissal by your current wage payer.

You do actually have a bit of leeway to 'adjust reality' in your CV. IDEA 38, *Bend the facts a little*, details areas where this is the case.

Try another idea...

Having said that, don't feel you have to provide an exhaustive guide to all the skeletons in your closet. Your CV really isn't the place to reveal that you hate the sight of your boss or that you haven't quite grasped the concept of punctuality! Simply weed out the weasel words.

**'Q: How can you tell when he's lying?
A: When his lips are moving.'**
Said of UK Prime Minister Harold Wilson in the 1960s satirical TV programme *That Was The Week That Was*

Defining idea...

How did
it go?

Q **I took your advice and took the unvarnished truth approach when putting a CV together for a job I really like the look of. However, I'm concerned that my CV will look a bit lightweight compared to those belonging to the shysters and bullshitters I'm up against. Have I done the right thing?**

A *Although I'm advocating telling the truth as opposed to lying in your CV, I'm quite comfortable with you telling the varnished truth as opposed to the unvarnished. It seems to me that the former is about presenting the truth positively and energetically, whereas the latter may easily look a bit, well, lacklustre.*

Q **Is it really that bad to use a bit of poetic licence?**

A *It's my belief that it's best not to fake anything. I'd contend that it's better to lose a job offer by being yourself than to receive an offer after pretending to be something you're not. If you've presented a distorted picture of who you are and what you want, you're likely to end up miserable in the job sooner or later.*

14

Numbers count

How to impress by numbers, using sales figures, savings, turnaround times and other relevant metrics.

Quantifying the business impact of your actions will do wonders in terms of impressing a potential employer.

Did you know that the Charge of the Light Brigade, generally regarded as a catastrophic British military blunder, was actually nothing of the sort? According to Terry Brighton, author of a book about the battle, some 60% of the men who took part returned 'without a scratch' and judged the encounter to be a success. I mention this not out of any revisionary zeal, but because I want to pick up on the phrase 'some 60% of the men who took part'. If instead of specifying '60%' the sentence stated 'quite a few' or 'the majority', would the sentence's meaning be conveyed as well? Let's face it, '60%' appears precise and unambiguous in a way that 'quite a few' most certainly isn't.

Now I know that numbers shouldn't necessarily be taken at face value either. It's sometimes said that there are three types of lies: lies, damned lies and statistics. Then of course there's that jibe that's often hurled at politicians, namely that they use statistics the way a drunk uses a lamp post – for support rather than illumination. However, these caveats aside, most people accept that numbers can carry a weight and conviction that mere words often struggle to emulate.

Here's an idea for you... **If you can't locate precise numbers to include in your CV, then guesstimate. After all, if *you* can't find accurate data, it's unlikely that anybody from the organisation you've applied to could prove you wrong.**

AVOID AMBIGUITY

Use as much quantification as possible and you'll give your CV genuine impact and authority. In contrast, there are words that can disguise a range of possible truths and these should be avoided at all costs. For example, what does it really mean when somebody writes that they 'manage a small team'? Assuming we're not talking *Snow White and the Seven Dwarfs* here, the unvarnished truth could be 'I manage 30 people', in which case you might be underselling yourself depending on how the reader interprets 'small', or it could be 'I share one admin assistant with two other people', in which case the phrase 'weasel words' pops to mind.

Another example is, 'I introduced a more efficient system for managing overtime and achieved a significant saving for the department.' Does that mean that the applicant saved 250,000 a year or thirty bucks?

QUANTIFICATION IS THE NAME OF THE GAME

Opportunities to use quantification include:

- The number of people employed by the company
- Company turnover
- Division turnover
- Size of budgets you were responsible for
- Number of people managed
- Money you've saved the organisation

- Improvements in turn-around times
- Improvements in productivity
- Improvements in levels of customer satisfaction
- Performance against sales targets
- Reduction in backlogs
- Achieving something against a tight timescale

You'll need to communicate these metrics with a bit of flair. More on this in IDEA 16, *Write with panache.*

Try another idea...

And here are four examples of quantified achievement statements:

1. Designed and successfully implemented a new set of shift rosters, reducing the department's wage bill by 12%.

'Round numbers are always false.'
SAMUEL JOHNSON

Defining idea...

2. Took over an ailing business and turned an annual loss of 8 million into a profit of 23 million within two years.

3. Exceeded sales target for the last financial year by 38%.

4. Increased the customer complaints dealt with within 24 hours from an average of 73% in 2003 to 98% in 2004.

Of course, in order to include some relevant metrics in your CV you'll need to have access to the data. So, if you don't already have these numbers to hand, now's a good time to start rummaging through the departmental filing system.

'To measure is to know.'
LORD BERKELEY, aristocrat and scientist

Defining idea...

How did
it go?

Q I've racked my brains and I'm struggling to come up with quantifiable information to put in my CV. Now what?

A   *It's not always easy to quantify our impact in our role. Before giving up entirely though, ask yourself first why your job exists and second what the output is from your job. Answering the first question will clarify your broad purpose. Answering the second should provide a clue about metrics. If your role is to process claims, how many do you process in a given period? If you serve in a shop, how many customers do you serve in a day and what are a typical day's takings? If you're a receptionist, how many people pass through your reception area? You may also find that the metrics in your work area don't operate at an individual level but rather at a team, departmental or organisational level. Somewhere around you there will be numbers, I promise!*

Q I've managed to come up with some numbers but frankly it's been a bad year for the company and they're not very impressive. Would I be better off keeping quiet?

A   *This problem often arises when trading conditions are difficult. It's easy enough to declare sales figures when they're up 18% on the previous year, but not so easy when they're down 18%. Even so, it can be worth putting your performance in context. If your numbers are down 18% against an industry average that's down 37%, then it's actually something to be proud of!*

15

Be an achiever

An impressive job description doesn't necessarily mean you're good at what you do. Far more meaningful is a substantial record of personal achievements.

Shortly after Gerald Ford succeeded Richard Nixon, one commentator said of the impact Ford had made: 'A year ago, he was unknown throughout America, now he's unknown throughout the world.'

You may also have heard the Woody Allen line that 90% of success at work is about turning up. Perhaps that was true a while back, but these days that attitude won't achieve survival, let alone success.

Potential employers are interested in what you actually do and (more critically) what difference you actually make rather than in what you're supposed to do. A CV that simply sets out a mini job description for all the roles you've held is therefore missing a trick.

Here's an idea for you... **Rate thirty or so achievements in terms of the likely impact they'll have on a recruiter. Ask yourself which are the strongest examples and aim to use those rather than their weaker counterparts.**

CVs have become increasingly achievement oriented in recent years. An achievement-based CV will give a potential employer a clear idea of the impact that you might have if recruited.

If you're planning to enter the job market in the near future you therefore need to be able to build into your CV an impressive set of achievements. By and large, though, we're pretty crap at recording our personal corporate triumphs. We tend to be a bit like one of those plucky British chaps in classic war movies who saves the entire regiment and then says in all modesty that he was only doing his job and there's no need to make a fuss as he still has one perfectly good leg left. In a similar way, we often don't give ourselves credit for the skills and abilities we have built up over the years and instead take them for granted.

Here's a quick exercise to help you see how good you are at recognising your achievements:

1. Write down thirty or so achievements that you're really proud of. If listing thirty achievements sounds excessive, please persevere. There's a tendency for people to do this exercise on automatic pilot to begin with. By the time you're up to achievement 23, you'll start surprising yourself with all you've done that had slipped from immediate recollection.

Defining idea...

'*Do, or do not. There is no try.*'
YODA, wise master of the Force and teacher of Jedi

2. Alongside each achievement, make a note of the underlying skills or abilities you drew on in order to succeed.

There's more on structuring achievement statements in IDEA 23, *Take the CAR*.

Try another idea...

Armed with the output from this exercise, you should get a pretty good idea of the skills and abilities you can take into the job marketplace.

Bear in mind that achievements are contextual; in other words, our work environment and the corporate culture that we're part of shape what's expected of us and what's possible for us to achieve. For example, you may have the capacity to be innovative yet work in an environment that's unsupportive of innovation, such as a risk-averse life assurance company. You may therefore struggle to come up with a work-based example of being innovative. Where this is the case and where you're putting yourself forward for a role that requires innovative thinking, you may need to provide an achievement that drew on innovation from either a previous role or from a non-work situation. It's perfectly legitimate to use such examples in your CV.

The downside with achievements is that – like much of your CV – they have a shelf life. A genuine achievement that goes back ten years or more won't carry as much of an impact as a more recent example will. I'm reminded of a quote that was allegedly printed on clothing worn by Britney Spears: 'I'm a virgin, but this is an old T-shirt.' But come what may, you'll need a demonstrable record of achievements in order to achieve your career ambitions. Without it, your marketability will plummet.

'Always drink upstream from the herd.'
WILL ROGERS, American humorist and actor

Defining idea...

How did
it go?

Q **Although I'm comfortable with expressing my work contribution in the form of achievement statements, how can I be sure these will match up with what my next employer (hopefully) is looking for?**

A *Sometimes we can be a bit literal in assessing the value of our achievements. Somebody selling encyclopedias door to door might focus on their sales figures, where they come in the sales league relative to colleagues and whether they've increased sales over the past year. Behind that performance there are a whole set of promotable skills. If the next employer (hopefully) is looking for characters with resilience, determination, self-motivation and good people skills, then it's perfectly possible that somebody selling encyclopedias could demonstrate those qualities extremely well.*

Q **I work in a very team-based environment so is it alright to concentrate on reporting team achievements?**

A *To a degree. Team-based achievements can indicate that you're a strong team player capable of working well with others. The trouble is that over-reliance on team-based content may obscure your individual contribution. Imagine you played in a football team and your team won the match 4–0. To a degree you could bathe in some reflected glory, but what if your sole contribution on the pitch was to concede a needless penalty, argue with the referee and get sent off after three minutes? That's why employers like to look behind team performance and get a glimpse of what you individually bring to the party. For that reason, do try to balance the team stuff with some of your personal attributes and strengths.*

16

Write with panache

Let's look at some ways to cut a linguistic dash and make a great impression.

Putting together a top-notch CV involves a balancing act between the conventions of CV writing and the need to try to stand out from the competition.

Emperor Charles V is probably best known for his remark: 'I speak Spanish to God, Italian to women, French to men and German to my horse.'

I repeat this remark not to upset my German readers, but to illustrate a core truth about the nature of effective communication: getting your message over is about adapting your approach to the needs to your audience.

As a general principle, you're more likely to stand out for content than style. That said, a stylistically inept CV will undermine even excellent content. And for that reason, it's important to observe the stylistic conventions of CV writing. Here are five useful habits to adopt:

Here's an idea for you...

Use the latest buzzwords. Being unaware of everyday phrases in a particular industry will show a lack of research on your part. Make yourself familiar with the latest business jargon, for example 'core competences' instead of skills. Avoid clichés like the plague!

Keep it snappy

You don't need to use complete sentences. Concise, understandable phrases are sufficient. No sentence fragments, however. They are very. Irritating. To read.

Loiter within tense

Aim to maintain a consistent approach to tense throughout. Most if not all of your CV should be written in the past tense. After all, the light dust of history has settled on all of your previous jobs. When you're describing the role you're in now, some elements will be current, such as the work you do on a day-to-day basis. Other parts will be in the past, however, such as the project you led that finished a few months ago or maybe last quarter's results. If you have a combination of present and past bullet-points to convey, cluster the present together and report them first. This may sound a bit finicky, but mixing them up just looks plain wrong.

Defining idea...

'Words, like Nature, half reveal And half conceal the Soul within.'
LORD TENNYSON, 'In Memoriam AHH'

Use the third person

Write about yourself in the third person rather than the first. This will lend an air of objectivity and professionalism to the proceedings that using 'I', 'me' and 'my' lacks.

Avoid confusing turns of phrase

I once received a CV from an applicant who claimed that he could 'fire people with enthusiasm'. He wasn't invited to interview and so I still don't know whether he meant that he was a superb motivator or that he could sack people with gusto. Check that you've expressed yourself as clearly as possible throughout. Even better, get someone else to have a read, as they'll spot things that would sail past you unchallenged.

For examples of words that will cut a dash, check out IDEA 25, Show some oomph.

Try another idea...

Don't try and be funny

You may have a take on life that's so amusing that your dinner party stories hospitalise accountants, but it's a different story when it comes to your CV. Humour depends on knowing your audience; you don't know the person who'll be assessing your CV so don't go there. And remember that puns are for children, not groan readers. (Sorry, couldn't resist it!)

Use plain English

In his 1946 essay 'Politics and the English Language', George Orwell came up with a set of six 'rules' for writing plainly and clearly. I think you'll agree they hold up very well as a set of principles for anybody writing their CV in the noughties:

'The play was a great success but the audience was a disaster.'
OSCAR WILDE

Defining idea...

1. Never use a metaphor, simile or other figure of speech that you're used to seeing in print.

2. Never use a long word where a short one will do.

3. If it's possible to cut a word out, always cut it out.

4. Never use the passive where you can use the active.

5. Never use a foreign phrase, a scientific word or a jargon word if you can think of an everyday English equivalent.

6. Break any of these rules sooner than say anything barbarous.

How did it go?

Q   Look, I'm no J.K. Rowling. If I was, I wouldn't be working for Scroggins Engineering, I'd be whooping it up with the literati in Cuba, wouldn't I?

A   *Point taken, but I'm not suggesting that having a successful corporate career depends on your gaining a Masters in Creative Writing. The techniques I'm talking about here come down to some straightforward, easy-to-follow guidelines.*

Q   OK, I get the basic idea – consistent tense, third person, plain language, no jokes and so on. Is that all there is to this one?

A   *Yes, but don't underestimate how difficult it is to write plainly and clearly. Quite often, we're our own worst judges when it comes to our writing. We think we've been the model of clarity and brevity, only to find that somebody reading our output gets confused about what we mean. The acid test of our writing isn't whether we think it's good, it's what other people make of it. To that end, and I know this is a bit of a recurring theme, I'd always recommend showing your CV and covering letter to a few people before you start sending it out.*

17
The seven deadly CV sins

**Sometimes best practice is about the things we do;
sometimes it's more about the things we don't do...**

The biggest CV sin is probably to bore
the pants off the reader, but there are
plenty of other pitfalls awaiting the inattentive
amongst us.

When we go in search of these pitfalls, do we find that the traditional seven deadly sins – Pride, Avarice, Envy, Wrath, Lust, Gluttony and Sloth – hold any lessons for the modern-day CV writer? Maybe, but some are admittedly more tenuous than others.

PRIDE

Pride can lead us to overstate our abilities. So, don't go describing your IT skills as 'excellent' when you know little more than how to turn on your PC. Equally, don't enclose a photo because you're damn good-looking, unless you're a model, actor or actress of course.

Here's an idea for you...

Avoid unnecessary repetition in your CV. Do not repeat things. Say them only once. Do not say them twice. Or three times. Once is enough. (Now can you see how irritating repetition is?)

AVARICE

Avarice can lead us to apply for jobs that are well beyond our capabilities. In truth, we're often more attracted to the salary than to the job itself.

The opposite of avarice is generosity. This means letting others have their fair share of praise. Don't therefore claim personal credit for a team achievement. Acknowledging the contributions of others from time to time will demonstrate that you can be a team player. On the other hand, don't 'we' all over your CV else you'll have the recruiter struggling to detect what you specifically bring to the party.

ENVY

Envy is about resenting the good others receive or the qualities they possess. In the context of CV writing, envy might come out in the form of sniping at the effort of others, which is a dangerous tactic. As a Russian proverb puts it, 'He who digs a hole for another may fall in it himself.'

Defining idea...

'Men are liars. We'll lie about lying if we have to. I'm an algebra liar. I figure two good lies make a positive.'
TIM ALLEN, US actor

Alternatively, we might feel tempted to claim experience and qualifications we don't possess in order to appear on an equal footing with others.

WRATH

Wrath is a furious level of anger that we'd like to vent on someone or something. If we've left or are leaving our current organisation on less than harmonious terms, maybe on the back of an acrimonious redundancy, there's a very human tendency to want to express those feelings. Just remember that your CV isn't the right place for this. It must remain a professional, dispassionate document – anything more emotive will do you more harm than good.

If you're still tempted by the thought of ever so slightly overstating the truth, go straight to IDEA 13, *Ditch the dodgy dossier*, for some honesty therapy.

Try another idea...

LUST

Lust is the self-destructive drive for pleasure out of proportion to its worth. Lust causes us to suspend rational judgement in the pursuit of gratification.

Remember that you're not obliged to accept the first job offer that comes your way. The offer may be flattering, but feel free to turn it down if it's a poor fit for the criteria you've set for your ideal job – salary level, degree of challenge in the role, location, future prospects and so on. On the other hand, when an offer meets most, but not all, of your criteria, you may choose to accept it or see if you can improve the offer through discussion.

'If you tell the truth you don't have to remember anything.'
MARK TWAIN

Defining idea...

Defining idea...

'Some rise by sin, and some by virtue fall.'
WILLIAM SHAKESPEARE

GLUTTONY

An overindulgent CV gives too much detail and goes on for too many pages.

An opposite of gluttony is moderation. The perfect CV gives the reader the right amount of information. Not too little to prevent the reader from really understanding what you have to offer. Equally not so much information that the reader is swamped with unnecessary detail.

SLOTH

Sloth is about an inclination to be lazy and to put in little effort. With CV writing, there are two areas where lack of effort will undermine success. The first is where we simply take our old CV and bring it up to date rather than going for a radical overhaul and rewrite. The second is where we don't put enough effort into adapting our CV for each job we apply for.

Q **I recently read a book called *Sin to Win*. Are you telling me sinning is back in the doghouse?**

How did it go?

A *In this case, yes. This idea is simply intended to reinforce the point that sometimes best practice is about the things we should do and sometimes about the things we shouldn't.*

Q **Is this a definitive list of sins?**

A *Absolutely not, but it's a reminder that some things definitely don't work well in your CV. Talking of which, in August 2004 a recruitment firm called Marketing Professionals came up with its own list of the top ten CV sins, namely:*

- *Typos – around 50% of CVs contain spelling mistakes or grammatical errors.*

- *Work experience listed in wrong order – recruiters recommend you put the most recent position first.*

- *Unexplained gaps in dates between jobs – if you've taken time off, you should say why.*

- *Sloppy formatting – using inappropriate fonts, mixing up styles and sizes, failing to align paragraphs or bullet points, etc.*

■ Trying to brighten things up with inappropriate use of colours, photographs, logos or fancy paper – this rarely puts you at the top of the pile.

■ Including irrelevant information such as holiday jobs or casual work.

■ Sending through a CV that has been constructed to apply for a different role – employers prefer a CV tailored to their vacancy.

■ A disorganised and hard-to-follow CV, with information scattered around the page.

■ Too much information – CVs should be kept to two or three pages and long paragraphs and sentences should be avoided.

■ Too little information – if it's too basic it won't interest the employer.

18

Looks can kill

Content is obviously important but so is presentation, so take the time to get it right.

If your CV is poorly presented, chances are that nobody will bother to read it. Here's some tips on how to present your CV both professionally and attractively.

Don't let this go any further, but I've reached the age where catching a glimpse of myself in a mirror first thing in the morning isn't a cheery experience. It's as though make-up artists from the *Lord of the Rings* wait until I fall asleep and spend the night producing a look that might be characterised as Orc with an attitude problem. The fact is, these days Middleton *au naturel* is a babe magnet to whom the iron filings of sexual attraction show a studied indifference. On the other hand, give me the time to doll myself up and I can walk freely in public places without scaring all but the most sensitive of souls.

You can probably see where this is leading in the context of high impact CVs. Elsewhere in this book we've looked at the importance of getting the language and tone of the CV right. But it's just as important for the look and layout to be easy on the reader's eye.

Here's an idea for you...

Choose just one font that's clear, distinct and easy to read, such as Arial, Times Roman, Verdana or Gill Sans. Using lots of different fonts will look messy.

THE KEY TO A GOOD-LOOKING CV

1. Your CV should be typed, of course. A handwritten version might show you're a quirky individualist, but most recruiters will regard you as somebody who either can't use or can't be bothered to gain access to a computer. Neither of these will endear a candidate to a company.

2. Use quality paper, typically white, which photocopies the best. There are those who swear by using tinted paper in the belief that this helps their CV catch the eye. Most recruiters, however, swear with equal force that this doesn't make a blind bit of difference. Whatever you do, don't go down the fluorescent pink route – it looks pug ugly and it's as though the paper is impregnated with a whiff of desperation.

3. Avoid front covers and fancy bindings. A recruiter wants to read your CV, not unwrap it! Pretentious packaging will almost certainly condemn your CV to the reject pile.

Defining idea...

'She got her good looks from her father: he's a plastic surgeon.'
GROUCHO MARX

4. Don't send out poor-quality photocopies of your CV, as this will give the impression that you're mailing your CV *en masse* and aren't too bothered who employs you.

5. Keep the content uncluttered. Edit it so that every line adds value. By ruthlessly excising extraneous information, you give yourself the opportunity to wrap lots of white space around the text. This looks good and is very handy for the recruiter to make notes on.

Still tempted to go for something a bit more flamboyant? IDEA 29, *Set the right tone*, should dispel any such career-damaging thoughts.

Try another idea...

6. Use bullet points, bold type, spacing, etc., to make the CV look as attractive and readable as possible. That said, don't ever just have a single bullet point, as this will look sloppy and inattentive.

7. Unless your CV is sponsored by Specsavers, keep your font size at around the 11 or 12 point mark. I've seen so many CVs where the writer has reduced the font size in order to cram as much information as possible into two sides of A4. It's not a pretty sight and predisposes the reader to earmark you for a 'no thanks' letter.

8. Watch out for typos and grammatical areas. Perhaps I'm old-fashioned, but my response to the person who scrawled 'You loosers' (*sic*) over the portrait of David Beckham at the Royal Academy in London, in response to the England football team's defeat in Euro 2004, was to castigate their spelling ability rather than applaud the sentiment expressed.

'People don't bat an eyelid about using moisturisers.'
JONNY WILKINSON, on life in the England rugby team's locker room, which demonstrates that appearance counts in the most unlikely settings

Defining idea...

87

How did it go?

Q I've just had another go at putting together my CV, incorporating some of this advice. I know that presentation is important but is all this really necessary?

A   When I cover this topic at CV writing workshops, there's invariably one wag who baulks at the idea that style is as important as substance, arguing that surely excellent content is the key thing to get right. They have a bit of a point – immaculately presented dross is unlikely to gain you an interview, whereas poorly presented but substantial content just might. It's a false argument though – far and away your best chance of securing an interview is for your CV to be both substantial and attractively presented.

Q OK, I'm prepared to be convinced that appearance makes a difference. What's the biggest blunder that we can make presentationally?

A   In my view, just about the biggest blunder is somebody sending their CVs out using their current employer's stationery and franking machine. Being regarded as somebody who steals office supplies is not the best recommendation to a new employer. In fact, I know recruiters who take such umbrage at that practice that, as soon as they realise what has happened, they bin or shred the envelope and contents.

19

Two CVs are better than one

Inside information on how to produce a tailor-made CV for each application.

Applying for jobs was different back in the 1980s. I remember one job-hunting phase where I sat at home listening to Frankie Goes to Hollywood while scouring the papers and cutting out any appealing job adverts.

Every time I found one, I'd take a CV from my pile of photocopies, pop it in an envelope, address the envelope, add a stamp and *voilà* – application to go. I used to time myself doing this; my unratified record was thirty-seven seconds.

To be fair, that particular approach was partly a product of the technology available back then. Changing your CV was a bit of a palaver, which typically involved gaining access to somebody with a manual typewriter or (if you were lucky) an early word processor the size of a fridge-freezer and trying to charm them into spending an hour of their time helping you to produce a new version.

Locate a couple of advertisements – one for the type of role you're currently filling and one in a new field that you'd be interested in. Put together a tailored version of your CV for each role, making sure that you highlight the key attributes you have to offer in each case.

These days, of course, pretty much everybody has access to a PC – almost certainly at work and probably at home – and so revising our CVs ought not to be beyond our wit and technological powers. This is just as well because just as the world has moved on since the 1980s, not to mention my musical taste, employers' expectations about the quality of CVs have risen sharply.

Nowadays, a CV isn't simply a statement of career experience to date, but a marketing document. And not just an ordinary marketing document either, but a *one-to-one* marketing document. What this means is that your CV needs to be customised to each and every job you apply for. To put it bluntly, if you're not producing a customised document every time your CV goes out, you're significantly reducing the likelihood of getting an interview.

Two key questions you need to ask yourself every time you put pen to paper are:

Defining idea...

'*The highest importance in the art of detection is to be able to recognise out of a number of facts which are incidental and which are vital.*'
SHERLOCK HOLMES

1. What does the organisation with the vacancy want?

2. What do I have to offer that matches what the organisation is looking for?

To take each in turn:

WHAT DOES THE ORGANISATION WITH THE VACANCY WANT?

This is fairly straightforward when the vacancy is advertised because all the information you need should be in the advertisement or contained in an information pack that the organisation will send you if you express an interest.

Where you've heard of the vacancy through the grapevine and there isn't a formal advertisement as such, you can still make an intelligent guess at the qualities required. If you can back that up with a chat with somebody who might give you some inside information on the vacancy, so much the better. Best of all, simply ring the manager with the vacancy directly to establish what they're after.

WHAT DO I HAVE TO OFFER THAT MATCHES WHAT THE ORGANISATION IS LOOKING FOR?

Show specifically how your experience matches the company's needs. If its advertisement asks for someone who's worked with younger staff and you've had experience of introducing three trainees into the department who've all gone on to be offered permanent positions, make sure you convey this.

If you've been able to speak to the manager with the vacancy, make sure that you've incorporated how you'd be able to meet their stated needs.

To delve more deeply into the art of interpreting job advertisements, turn to IDEA 11, *Reading the runes.*

Try another idea...

How did it go?

Q **I'm really struggling with this 'one-to-one marketing document' concept. Are you telling me there's no place for old-school CVs?**

A *As far as I'm concerned, the old-school CV has gone the way of Sinclair C5s and Betamax. If you've no idea what I'm talking about, then I think I've made my point! If you do remember, then you've been around long enough to know that life moves on. New technologies make new things possible. These days, most of us have ready access to a PC and internet connection. As a result, it's never been easier to create, update and store documents, plus quality research into companies is now only a search engine away. As soon as a few people realised they could outpace the competition by producing specific CVs for specific jobs, job-hunting entered a new era.*

Q **Alright, I accept that standards have risen, but surely when the job market is tight and there are fewer people looking to move jobs, employers can't afford to be too picky, can they?**

A *You're right to say that a tight job market typically means fewer applicants. There's no real evidence, however, that employers have to drop their standards. If there are only ten applicants but nine CVs are better than yours, you're likely to end up on the 'reserve' pile at best.*

20

How to deal with the skeletons in your CV

Want to know how to mind the gaps in your CV or a track record that'd qualify you for membership of Job-hoppers Anonymous?

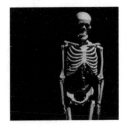

In an ideal world, we'd all have unimpeachable working histories and picture-perfect CVs. In reality, we may have a skeleton (or at least a metatarsal) or two in the career closet.

Here are two slightly tricky career scenarios that you may have to deal with:

GAPS

The year you took off to write your as yet unpublished novel, the six months you spent bumming around the world or that decade when you just didn't feel like working – many of us have acquired gaps in our career history. Although there's a tendency to assume that employers will see these gaps as negative, that's not always the case.

Here's an idea for you... **Review your job history, and go over any elements that you aren't currently comfortable with talking about. Any discomfort on your part will be picked up by a professional interviewer, so develop a storyline that you feel comfortable with.**

The absolute golden rule is not to leave a gap in your CV unaccounted for. Recruiters who notice gaps such as these are likely to think the applicant is less honest than average. On the other hand, if recruiters notice a gap for which an explanation is provided, then the applicant is typically thought to be more honest than average.

There's also some evidence to show that it's possible to really turn gaps between jobs to your advantage. The trick is to be very positive about both what you did and what you got out of it. If you're able to identify job-relevant skills that you picked up along the way, then you have no worries.

JOB-HOPPING

Let's say that you have a career history that would have qualified you for Job-hopper of the Year several years running. For temporary roles, this normally won't be a problem because you'll simply be maintaining an already established pattern. If you're applying for a permanent job, however, there are things you can do to make the most of your colourful past so that you're not seen as a corporate commitment-phobe.

Defining idea... *'Don't be afraid to give your best to what seemingly are small jobs. Every time you conquer one it makes you that much stronger. If you do the little jobs well, the big ones tend to take care of themselves.'*
DALE CARNEGIE

The key to success is to present your career using a functional CV format. This type of CV, as you may remember from earlier, focuses on skills and achievements in contrast to the reverse chronological model that emphasises each individual role you've held.

If you're more concerned about your age than your career history, IDEA 26, *Act your age*, is the one for you.

Try another idea...

Using a functional approach, you can devote the first page of your CV to drawing relevant information from across the full range of jobs you've held. Place this evidence under headings that are relevant to the vacancy you're applying for, such as decision-making, handling customers, team working, etc. Employers will expect to see a job history somewhere on your CV, but by putting it on page two you'll be downplaying its significance a bit.

REMEMBER ABRAHAM LINCOLN

You may find that some employers will decline the opportunity to give you a job despite your very best presentational efforts. Risk-averse organisations whose natural preference is for stolid, dull, unadventurous recruits may find your past just a bit too colourful. Then again, would you really want a job in those types of place?

It's worth remembering that persistence will pay off as long as you keep throwing your CV hat into the employment ring. Not only will it pay off, but it may yield spectacularly good

'Whatever you are, be a good one.'
ABRAHAM LINCOLN

Defining idea...

results over the long term. US President Abraham Lincoln had many a setback in his life and career as the following record shows:

1832   Defeated in the race for the legislature
1833   Failed in business
1834   Elected to legislature
1835   Sweetheart died
1836   Suffered a nervous breakdown
1838   Defeated for speaker in the legislature
1843   Defeated for nomination to Congress
1846   Elected to Congress
1848   Lost renomination
1849   Rejected for job as land officer
1854   Defeated for Senate
1856   Defeated for nomination for vice-president
1858   Defeated for Senate
1860   Elected sixteenth president of the United States

So, take comfort from Abe's CV and don't ever give up.

Q   **I've had many jobs over the past five years, but now I've decided I want to take my career a bit more seriously and find some long-term employment. What's the best way to present my errant past?**

How did it go?

A   *Don't present a comprehensive list showing how you spent two months here or three months there. Instead, consider rolling them all up under one heading along the lines of: '1999–2004: Various temporary roles'. In order to convince an employer that you're now a safe recruitment bet you'll need to explain why you held so many temporary roles and why you haven't sought a permanent role until now. For example: 'During this period, I was a member of a semi-professional band that regularly toured the UK, making it impractical to take on a permanent role. The band split up in late 2003.'*

Q   **That's helpful. Are there any other strategies I could use?**

A   *You may also find that you can cluster jobs into related groups. For example, if you worked in eight restaurants over a two-year period, rather than list the individual restaurants and the periods you spent at each one, you could soften things by writing it up along the following lines: '1999–2001: Various front of house roles in clubs and restaurants. During this period, I took a number of temporary roles working in places like McDonald's, TGI Fridays and Stringfellows. These jobs helped me to develop a high level of confidence in dealing with customers, sometimes in situations that required high levels of tact and diplomacy.'*

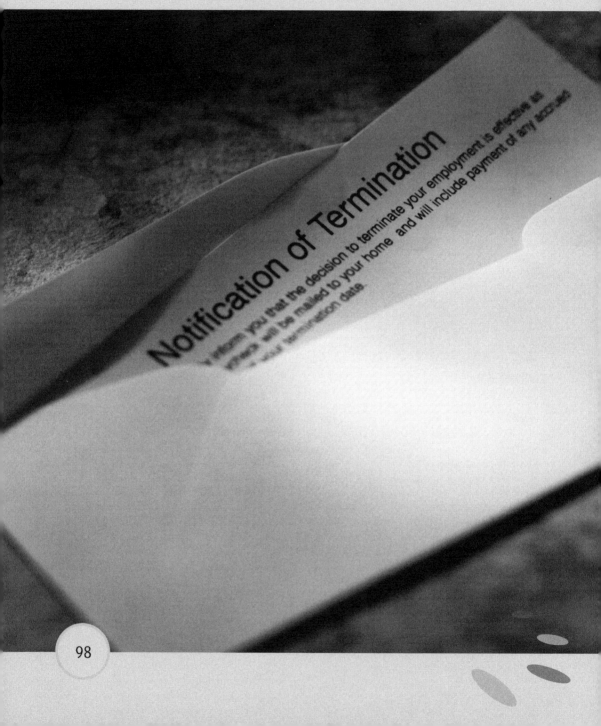

21

Another skeleton, another cupboard: redundancy

Redundancy isn't the show-stopper it once was, but you still need to be careful how you convey this news to an interviewer.

Being made redundant used to be an unmentionable topic. These days we're more accustomed to it, but there are still at least two lingering myths about its significance.

MYTH 1: THEY BROUGHT IT ON THEMSELVES

Back in the strife-ridden 1970s, some companies would use redundancy programmes as an opportunity to give troublemakers, ne'er-do-wells and social misfits the chop. Consequently, anyone made redundant found themselves regarded with some suspicion by the job market, even when the real problem was more likely to be incompetent management that left companies in financial doo-doo.

Here's an idea for you... **When explaining the background to your redundancy, avoid any hint of negativity and never contemplate using the phrase 'personality clash' as that'll give the recruiter the willies and ensure you don't make the shortlist. Try rehearsing your answer. Why not test it out on a sympathetic ear?**

Not any more. Redundancy has become commonplace. The vast majority of redundancies come about on the back of a downturn in business, restructuring within a business or mergers. Against this backdrop, most people who are made redundant are simply in the wrong role at the wrong time.

MYTH 2: IT'S EASIER TO GET A JOB FROM A JOB

Jobseekers seem to think that employers are better disposed to applicants with jobs and that applicants are at a disadvantage if they're on the market due to redundancy. Again, not true. Statistically there's no evidence to back this up.

These days, most recruiters pay little heed to redundancy when assessing the suitability of a candidate. In fact, quite a few recruiters regard it as a positive because it means that the individual is definitely in play, as opposed to applying for other jobs as a means of leveraging a better deal back at the ranch. It also means that the applicant is likely to be available at short notice.

HERE'S THE DEAL

There really isn't any stigma attached to redundancy anymore, as long as you effectively manage how you pass on this news. The key is to come up with an explanation in your covering letter that makes you sound professional and positive about losing your job.

Is there any merit in keeping quiet? I don't think so and here's one reason why:

Now start thinking about the bigger picture by turning to **IDEA 49, *Managing the brand called You.***

Try another idea...

Imagine you've applied for a job and been invited to an interview. Up comes the inevitable question, 'Why are you looking to move on from your current role?' You explain that you've been made redundant. A look of surprise is followed by a puzzled frown from the interviewer, who scans your CV and covering letter to see if they missed something. This isn't good news because the interviewer now has a sense that you haven't been entirely open in your CV, which will lead them to speculate what else you haven't disclosed.

So, my unambiguous advice is to come clean, presenting the most positive spin that you can. Here's one example of how you might convey the news in your letter: 'Following a restructuring of the business, the entire European division was closed down and I was one of thirty people affected. I was offered a role elsewhere in the company, but have decided that the time is right to seek out a role in a company that can offer me...'

'It's a recession when your neighbor loses his job; it's a depression when you lose your own.'
HARRY S. TRUMAN

Defining idea...

You'll have your own variation of the facts, of course. Just make sure that you demonstrate your stoic quality.

'Always bear in mind that your own resolution to succeed is more important than any other one thing.'
ABRAHAM LINCOLN

Defining idea...

101

How did it go?

Q **I'm surprised you say that most recruiters pay little heed to redundancy. I've been advised that I shouldn't mention the 'R' word until I'm being interviewed. Is this incorrect?**

A *It's true that a few career advisers still act as though there's something vaguely shameful about being 'let go'. According to their view of the job market, if you're unemployed or have been made redundant, you shouldn't mention it in your initial approach for fear it might put a potential employer off. In my opinion, that's total nonsense. For the past seven years, I've worked with people who've been made redundant and I've yet to come across a case where it looked like declaring the redundancy in the CV or covering letter did any harm. And I know plenty of recruiters who are adamant that they'd prefer to know and that it's not regarded as a detrimental factor.*

Q **Now that I've been made redundant, is there anything else I should be doing?**

A *If you can secure some outplacement support as part of your leaving package, grab it. It will be particularly helpful if it's been a few years since you were last active in the external job market. There are some excellent providers in the outplacement market who'll help you think through what needs to go into your CV, critique your early drafts, give you some interview practice and generally help you tune up for the marketplace.*

22

Selling a one-company career

It is possible to convey a one-company career to your advantage without suggesting that you're boring or lacking in ambition (even if you are).

After all, it wasn't that far back in the corporate timeline when change used to happen in bursts, if at all.

Occasionally, a new CEO would turn up on the doorstep, have a rush of blood to the head and personally redesign the business on the back of attending an executive seminar. Senior managers would sigh, brace themselves for a few bumpy months and look forward to a time when life in the company would settle down again.

Then, in the mid- to late 1980s, companies realised they'd have to flick the change switch onto constant and things have never been the same since. These days, constant change is an unquestioned given on most corporate agendas.

Here's an idea for you...

Find some positive adjectives to describe yourself. You have every right to play up the fact that you're 'committed', 'professional', 'experienced' and a 'team contributor'.

What's all this got to do with how to present a one-company career in your CV? Quite simply this. It used to be the case that in terms of experience a twenty-five year stint with one organisation was likely to amount to one year lived twenty-five times over. When the pace of change was low, there was little need for organisations to substantially change their operating patterns and as a result roles in the company tended to be about delivering a consistent performance year in and out. Staff turnover stayed fairly low and opportunities for personal growth and development were limited for many.

Over the last fifteen to twenty years, that situation has changed markedly. Driven by factors like global competition and developments in information technology, companies now expect a much higher level of flexibility and adaptability from their staff.

It has admittedly become less common for people to spend such long periods with one company, but those who do choose to stay (or just forget to leave) do have a plausible and convincing storyline to present to potential employers.

The key is to assemble your CV in such a way that it shows good progression within the company and a track record of acquiring new skills. In terms of presentation, put the most emphasis on what you've been doing over the last four to six years. And if you've had more than six roles in the company, don't list every single role and describe key responsibilities for each. The roles that you filled in the 1970s and

80s are unlikely to score many brownie points with the typical 21st-century recruiter. Instead, you might do well to wrap up that period into a catch-all couple of sentences. Possibly something along the lines of: 'EARLY CAREER: Shortly after joining Scroggins Engineering in 19XX as a junior accounts clerk, I was transferred onto the junior management development programme. I went on to achieve a number of promotions before being appointed to the role of Finance Manager in 19XX.'

Quantify your achievements to demonstrate the impact you've had in your organisation. For more on this see IDEA 14, Numbers count.

Try another idea...

OK, time for a quick reality check. There will be companies that won't take your application seriously simply because of your high level of corporate fidelity. If they're convinced that they want a young, ambitious and dynamic person, they might well think that they're unlikely to detect those qualities in a career trajectory that shows solid and steady progression over a number of years. Bizarrely, this has little to do with an applicant's actual qualities and more to do with unshiftable stereotypes.

Generally though, if you set about describing your career positively, emphasising everything you've achieved, there's no reason why your CV should pale in comparison with any of the job-hopping competition.

'Individual commitment to a group effort – that is what makes a team work, a company work, a society work, a civilization work.'
VINCE LOMBARDI, American football coach

Defining idea...

How did
it go?

Q   **I've applied for several jobs that I felt I was very well suited to,
but I've not yet had a single interview. Am I doing something
wrong?**

A   *Not necessarily. It may just be the state of the market. That said, it's always
possible that your CV is letting you down. The most important thing is to
focus on what you've been doing over the last four to six years. Don't give
equal weight to all your jobs – this is a CV, not an attempt to set out a
balanced and proportionate picture of your life to date. The fact that you
held a particular role for ten years back in the 1980s and early 1990s
doesn't merit the role getting more than three or four lines at the most,
even if it was the best job you ever had. It may have been a good time for
you, but it's past it sell-by date in the CV world.*

Q   **Anything else I should watch out for?**

A   *Nothing specific. But do watch out for any elements that counter any
suggestion that you're a dried out organisational husk. Make your CV
achievement-oriented; use positive, enthusiastic language; and include a
profile statement to give your CV a more contemporary look.*

23

Take the CAR

When it comes to work, simply being there isn't enough. We need to achieve some good outcomes for the company at the same time.

You must have come across them — those selfless, unassuming, committed and dedicated individuals who exist in varying numbers in just about every company.

You know, the ones that concentrate on doing the best possible job they can, claiming no credit and paying no real heed to ensuring that the company acknowledges their contribution. They finish one task, maybe allow themselves just a fleeting moment of personal satisfaction and then quietly move on to the next task on their list.

At one level, there's something admirable about them. But as somebody who spends quite a bit of his time counselling people who've been made redundant, I know it's often these self-effacing, highly capable and loyal employees who are the first to be 'let go'. If nobody knows how good you really are, why would your company expect to miss you if you weren't around any more? The irony is that these people almost invariably have some solid tangible achievements under their belts. They just never let on.

Here's an idea for you... **Mix and match how you report your achievements. Take one of your achievements, try reproducing it in all three forms (CAR, AR and RA) and see which to you seems to have the strongest impact.**

We, of course, wouldn't fall into the same trap. We know that our career trajectory is only partly determined by what we do and that it's equally important that we can represent our achievements to others. Not in a deeply unpleasant Me Me Me boasting-at-the-bar way, but rather in a tone of quiet pride.

THE CAR

When it comes to depicting our achievements, both in writing and face to face, there's a structured approach that's used widely in outplacement and recruitment consultancies to help people structure their thinking about their achievements in the workplace. It's called the CAR model and it goes like this:

Challenge: the backdrop to the situation; the situation that existed before you took some action.
Action: what you did specifically to address the challenge.
Result: the business impact of your actions.

Here's a (slightly fanciful) example of the CAR model in action:

Challenge: When I first joined the organisation as Finance Manager, morale in the department was at rock bottom.
Action: Once a week, I went to work dressed as a well-known cartoon character. Every Friday afternoon, I personally served all members of the department with a variety of non-alcoholic cocktails.

Result: Morale in the department soared. The company's annual staff surveys show consistent year-on-year improvement in levels of job satisfaction within the department for each of the three years I worked there.

Achievements are important, but so is your softer side. Try IDEA 28, *I'm keen on ping pong, playing the ukulele and going to the theatre*, for tips on how to get your wider qualities across.

Try another idea...

When we go along to an interview, the CAR model provides a useful framework for describing our organisational impact.

When writing our CV, we might sometimes drop the Challenge element as a means of saving space and in order to really emphasise our impact. Technically I suppose, this should be called the AR model.

AR versus RA
We can also subtly change the impact of our achievement statements depending on how we choose to sequence information. There can be a world of difference between an AR sequence and an RA sequence. Consider these two variations on the same achievement:

AR: Ran thirty one-day workshops on the theme of eliminating waste, which generated savings of £2m for the company.

RA: Generated savings for the company of two million as a result of running thirty one-day workshops on the theme of eliminating waste.

'Achievement seems to be connected with action. Successful men and women keep moving. They make mistakes, but they don't quit.'
CONRAD HILTON, founder of the international chain of business hotels that bear his name

Defining idea...

109

Defining idea... **'I am always doing things I can't do. That's how I get to do them.'**
PABLO PICASSO

Now you might think I'm disappearing up my own semantic rear here, but to me the first example emphasises the technical contribution made (i.e. the running of the workshops) while the second example highlights business impact and seems to demonstrate a more organisation-focused outlook.

How did it go?

Q I'm one of those people who prefers to just get on with the job. I've been staring at a blank sheet of paper for half an hour trying to come up with some achievements. Any ideas?

A *Often the issue with the more modest of us isn't that we don't have any achievements to speak of. It's more that we don't really take that much notice of them when they happen.*

Q Fair diagnosis I suspect, but what can I do about it?

A *See if these questions bring any of your achievements back to the surface:*

1. *What can you do better than other people in your area?*
2. *How often were you promoted?*
3. *When did you last show some initiative?*
4. *And the time before that?*
5. *Have you ever won an award (e.g. Team Leader of the Month)?*

6. Did you generally get good performance reviews? What do people say about you?
7. Ever received thank you letters from customers or colleagues?
8. Have you ever produced anything tangible (like a newsletter) on a regular basis?
9. Or as a one-off?
10. Have you ever managed a project that finished on time and within budget?
11. Or been involved in a project as a team member? What happened?
12. Have you ever suggested improvements that have been implemented? Did they work?
13. Ever got involved with the employee suggestion scheme?
14. Have you ever saved the company time or money?
15. Have you ever improved a turnaround time?
16. Have you ever reduced backlogs in your part of the business?

I'm sure there are other worthwhile questions, but hopefully these will have given you a decent start.

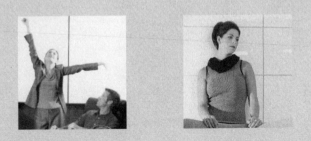

24

Corporate prehistory

It's said that actors are only as good as their last performance. Rather alarmingly, the same principle applies in corporate life, meaning much of your experience is already past its sell-by date.

In 1997, Tony Blair led the UK Labour Party back into power, Princess Diana died, Hong Kong was handed back to China and the Spice Girls released their classic first album. The question is, what were you up to career-wise seven years ago?

Perhaps you were working or maybe you were still at school or college. Depending on your age, 1997 might seem like an age ago or it might seem like the day before yesterday. From an employer's perspective, it's almost certainly too long ago to matter.

Most employers would reckon that what you've been up to over the past three to five years is the best indicator of your potential level of contribution over the next

Here's an idea for you... **Think about something to report from your personal life that could impress the person who could be your next boss. A non-work achievement from last year probably has more relevance and impact than a work-based achievement of ten years ago.**

three to five years. For that reason, they'll be particularly attentive to the chunk of your CV covering that period. There is a certain logic to this viewpoint. If you've had a traditional career trajectory, then the chances are that your current or most recent role represents the pinnacle of your career to date, as measured by seniority and level of responsibility. Therefore, most of the strongest examples and evidence you might want to present to a potential employer are likely to be drawn from the recent past.

If, in contrast, you find yourself dredging up an example from 1997 to demonstrate your experience at, say, project management, and that's your most recent example, what is a potential employer likely to make of that? Surveys suggest that they might well take the view that your project management skills are a shade rusty, to put it kindly. So, if you have a more up-to-date example, you should always use it in preference to something of older vintage.

This explains why a typical CV representing a typical career progression devotes the most amount of space to the most recent role, with the role before that taking up a little less space and the role before that getting

Defining idea... *'Intellectual property has the shelf life of a banana.'*
BILL GATES

less space again. And so on, until your early career may well be represented by a simple one-line statement of job title, company name and the dates you worked there.

You might think that it's hardly worth mentioning a job in such sparse detail, but it can serve a purpose. Sometimes a CV can demonstrate a strong sense of career progression (for example, a series of jobs held that developed over time from Clerical Assistant to Clerical Officer to Executive Officer to Assistant Manager to Manager to Senior Manager to Assistant Director) simply by reference to the job titles you've held over the years.

For more on how to excise value-diminishing content from your CV, nip along sharply to IDEA 8, Cut to the chase.

Try another idea...

As a rough guide, this is how you might want to present your career experience:

- **Current role** Description of role followed by six to eight bullet points covering key responsibilities and achievements.

- **Previous role** As above, but with four to six bullet points.

- **Role before that** Three to four bullet points.

- **And the role before that** Two to three bullet points.

There are, as ever, exceptions to this principle. Say that you've been in your current role for a year and the role before that for ten years. Given the amount of time you were in the previous role, it would be reasonable to devote at least the same amount of space to that role as to your current position.

'*In the industrial age, information was like gold. In the digital age, it is like milk – use it quickly.*'
Consultancy NUA's advertising slogan in the 1990s

Defining idea...

115

The key to success with this idea is to use your common sense. As a general principle though, concentrate on drawing examples and evidence from the present and most recent past.

How did it go?

Q   I've been trying to put together a job application. However, I can't meet some of the things they're asking for in terms of experience without going back to jobs I had over twelve years ago. Is that really too long ago to include?

A   *Actually, an old example can be better than no example, but bear in mind that some experience travels the years better than other experience. For example, if the company are looking for somebody who can lead a team, they'd probably want the ideal candidate to have had very recent experience of managing people. If you haven't led a team since 1994, the company might legitimately wonder why that should be the case and whether your leadership skills are too rusty to be trusted. On the other hand, imagine that the company wants somebody with a high commitment to quality. If back in 1994 you led your team to achieving a formal quality standard and you had no more recent example, it would be highly relevant to mention this even though it was over a decade ago.*

Q   If most of my relevant experience is ancient history, what's the best approach for my CV?

A   *This might be a good opportunity to use a functional CV because it largely ignores chronology and puts the focus instead on your relevant skills and abilities.*

25

Show some oomph

Don't let your CV become an acronym for 'Characterless Verbalese'. Instead, use positive, active language to convey enthusiasm and make yourself (even) more interesting.

Only apply for a job if you think you can do it and if you find the prospect exciting. You need the right qualifications, of course, but a sizeable dollop of enthusiasm and commitment is equally important.

However, conveying this can be a linguistic challenge: in essence, your CV is just a bunch of words. It's one thing for you to exude in the flesh enthusiasm and commitment to take on a new role, but it's something entirely different to be able to communicate those qualities in writing.

When we write a CV, there's a curious tendency for some of us to use very formal, stiff language to convey information. For example, we slip into the passive tense ('It

Here's an idea for you... **Pick out, say, twenty action verbs and ten personal qualities. Choose words that have the strongest impact on you then try to incorporate them into the next draft of your CV, with the vast majority on page one. Finally, compare this new draft with the previous version. Which do you prefer?**

is anticipated that savings in excess of 5,000 will be generated...'). Alternatively, we use action verbs and adjectives to describe our personal characteristics that seem to fit the bill but nonetheless manage to sound tired and clapped out. You know the sort of thing – proactive, self-starter, team player, target-driven or man-manager (which in a mere ten letters and a hyphen manages to imply that the writer is behind the times and implicitly sexist).

What we need to spice up our CVs are words with a bit of semantic oomph that haven't yet been seconded to the lexicon of management clichés. With this in mind, I've had a bash at putting together a list of action verbs and adjectives that convey personal characteristics. Some of the latter might fit well in your profile statement or your covering letter. These aren't comprehensive lists and certainly won't be putting the *Oxford English Dictionary* out of business, but hopefully you'll find a few words to enliven your CV a smidgen. Feel free to add any other words that you think will do the business.

ACTION VERBS

Accelerated
Accomplished
Achieved
Actioned
Analysed
Appointed
Appraised
Approved
Audited
Balanced
Budgeted
Built
Captured
Centralised
Changed
Collaborated
Collected
Communicated
Completed
Conducted
Consulted
Controlled
Converted
Created
Decided

Defined
Delivered
Demonstrated
Designed
Determined
Developed
Devised
Diagnosed
Directed
Displayed
Documented
Doubled
Earned
Edited
Educated
Encouraged
Engineered
Enhanced
Established
Estimated
Evaluated
Examined
Exceeded
Executed
Expanded

Powerful language is important but IDEA 10, *Learn to speak 'behaviourese'*, shows you still need to craft it into a format that'll have high impact.

Extracted
Facilitated
Finalised
Financed
Finished
Forecast
Formed
Generated
Guaranteed
Guided
Halved
Handled
Headed
Helped
Hired
Identified
Implemented
Improved
Improvised
Increased
Influenced

Try another idea...

Initiated
Inspired
Installed
Instigated
Interviewed
Introduced
Invented
Invested
Investigated
Judged
Launched
Learned
Lectured
Led
Liaised
Lowered
Made
Maintained
Managed
Manipulated
Mapped
Marketed
Matched
Maximised
Mediated
Met
Minimised

Monitored
Motivated
Mounted
Navigated
Negotiated
Obtained
Offered
Opened
Operated
Optimised
Ordered
Organised
Overcame
Oversaw
Participated
Performed
Persuaded
Piloted
Pioneered
Planned
Positioned
Predicted
Prepared
Prescribed
Presented
Prevented
Processed

Produced
Projected
Promoted
Proposed
Provided
Published
Purchased
Quadrupled
Qualified
Quantified
Raised
Realised
Rearranged
Recommended
Reconciled
Reconstructed
Recruited
Rectified
Redesigned
Redirected
Reduced
Referred
Refined
Regulated
Reinforced
Reinvigorated
Renewed

Reorganised
Repaired
Replaced
Reported
Rescued
Researched
Resolved
Responded
Restored
Restructured
Retained
Reviewed
Revitalised
Revised
Revived
Revolutionised
Salvaged
Satisfied
Saved
Scheduled
Secured
Selected
Set up
Sold
Solved
Specified
Stabilised

Staffed
Standardised
Started
Stemmed
Stopped
Streamlined
Strengthened
Stretched
Structured
Studied
Submitted
Succeeded
Suggested
Summarised
Supervised
Supplemented
Supplied
Tailored
Taught
Terminated
Tested
Tightened
Traced
Tracked
Traded
Trained
Transformed

'I think most of us are looking for a calling, not a job. Most of us, like the assembly line worker, have jobs that are too small for our spirit. Jobs are not big enough for people.'
NORA WATSON, from the book *Working* by Studs Terkel

Tripled
Uncovered
Undertook
Unified
United
Updated
Upgraded
Verified
Widened
Won
Worked
Wrote

Defining
idea...

121

PERSONAL QUALITIES

Accountable	Experienced	Reliable
Adaptable	Flexible	Resilient
Analytical	Innovative	Resourceful
Articulate	Insightful	Results-focused
Autonomous	Intuitive	Risk-taking
Challenging	Leading edge	Self-motivated
Clear thinking	Logical	Skilled
Committed	Open	Straightforward
Conceptual	Organised	Supportive
Confident	Perceptive	Talented
Creative	Polished	Team player
Dynamic	Pragmatic	Thorough
Effective	Productive	Versatile
Energetic	Professional	

I hope that that little lot will provide you with a decent basis for energising the language used in your CV. That's if you can be bothered, of course. You might prefer to be a proactive self-starter.

Defining idea...

'*Nothing great was ever achieved without enthusiasm.*'
RALPH WALDO EMERSON

Q   It seems to me that some words carry more clout than others. Is there a hierarchy of impact?

How did it go?

A   *What a question! I've not seen a top ten list for either classification, but it's an intriguing thought. Actually, if they were to exist, the main drawback would be that the top ten words would quickly become clichés through excess use. That aside, a word like 'implemented' obviously carries more weight than, say, 'suggested', and a word like 'created' is a bit more impressive than 'revised'. However, if you're in a role that involves suggesting and revising rather than implementing and creating, then although the distinction may be interesting, it'd only be academic.*

Q   Do you have any more suggestions regarding how best to use these lists?

A   *A useful exercise is to highlight all the action verbs and personal qualities used in your draft CV and then try to come up with stronger alternatives using the lists featured in this section.*

26

Act your age

Is it better to disclose your date of birth or to keep it under your hat?

Whether it's Tiger Woods winning golf tournaments at twenty-one, Maria Sharapova conquering Wimbledon at seventeen or Lulu roaring up the 1960s charts with 'Shout' at fourteen, there's definitely something impressive about young achievers.

But as night follows day, so the years roll by for all of us. When it comes to our working lives, is there an ideal age to gain access to the maximum number of opportunities? An old HR colleague of mine used to say that companies would be happy to populate themselves entirely with 35-year-old managers with MBAs if there were enough to go around. His view used to strike me as a little overstated, although funnily enough I did come across a report earlier this year called 'Too young at 35, too old at 40 – ageism in the British workplace'.

Here's an idea for you... **Don't feature your age on page one of your CV. Instead, place it near the bottom of page two to give you an opportunity to present your argument for being interviewed, including all your relevant experience, before your age becomes any kind of consideration.**

According to this report, which was published by the Chartered Institute of Personnel and Development (CIPD), ageism is so rife in the British workplace that people have just five years – between the age of 35 and 40 – during which they're unlikely to be judged too young or too old for a job. The CIPD evidence, endorsed by similar findings from the Department for Work and Pensions, also found that age prejudice is much worse for people aged over 40, with over a third of workers over 50 claiming to have experienced age discrimination at work.

Within two years, British employers will be acting illegally if they let age prejudice influence their recruitment. The CIPD warns employers that they need to start changing their ways immediately instead of waiting for the government to implement legislation from Europe in 2006. In the meantime, how should we decide whether or not to state our age on our CV? Well, no matter what age you are, from my experience of working with recruitment managers and line managers I'd recommend stating your age explicitly.

Defining idea... **'The rewards of ageing always seem to slightly outweigh the freshness of youth.'**
DOUGLAS COUPLAND, novelist

If you're aged under 40, then you've little to be worried about in terms of your age itself. You will, however, need to be alert to the 'experience required' trap. Recruiters tend not to state an ideal age range any more, preferring to go for the more subtle approach of outlining the number of years' experience the successful candidate is likely to have. The message is the same though. A 25-year-old is unlikely to have, say, ten years' experience of any work-related skills. All you can do in response to this type of requirement is to have a CV jam-packed with as much high-quality experience as you can muster and hope that quality will outweigh quantity. But even in this circumstance, withholding your age serves no positive purpose.

So, honesty is important in a CV yet rigid adherence to the facts isn't. Reconcile these two statements at IDEA 38, *Bend the facts a little.*

Try another idea...

If you are aged 40 or over and you don't state your age, recruiters will try to establish your age from other available information, such as the dates you took certain exams. Actually, research seems to show that when recruiters try to estimate the age of an applicant who hasn't given their date of birth, they tend to overestimate the candidate's age by an average of two to three years. So paradoxically, not supplying our age because we're concerned that we might be regarded as too old can actually result in recruiters imagining we're even older than we really are!

'Age is not a particularly interesting subject. Anyone can get old. All you have to do is live long enough.'
GROUCHO MARX

Defining idea...

127

How did
it go?

Q   I've just seen an advertisement for a job I'd love to apply for. The only catch is that the ad is asking for people with three to five years' working experience and I have twenty-five. Do I stand a hope in hell's chance of getting the job?

A   *It's hard to say. Certainly the advertisement is implying that the ideal candidate is likely to be twenty-something rather than forty-something. Still, if you believe you meet all other job requirements in terms of experience and qualifications I'd say give it a go. Aside from the time involved in putting a CV and covering letter together and the cost of postage, what do you really have to lose? Remember not to reveal your age at the very beginning of your CV because if the recruiters are indeed set on hiring a younger person, they're more likely to dismiss your CV precipitately if it's immediately apparent to them that you in your forties. If, on the other hand, you hold the information back until the bottom of the second page there's a better chance you'll at least be able to make a decent pitch for the job.*

Q   Isn't discrimination on grounds of age illegal these days?

A   *It's certainly illegal in parts of America – California, for instance – but in the UK there's currently no direct statutory provision giving protection from discrimination on the grounds of age. However, the European Council passed the Equal Treatment Framework Directive in November 2000, following which all European member countries will be required to implement national legislation prohibiting discrimination on the grounds of age by 2006. Currently anybody who believes they've been treated less favourably for a reason relating to their age would have to link this to another form of discrimination, such as sex discrimination.*

27

Bob versus Robert

An interviewer can legitimately quote anything in your CV back at you. So, I suggest you use the name you want to be called by.

Your wife calls you Bob. Your work colleagues call you Bob. All your mates down the pub call you Bob. This would obviously be a tad galling if your name is Richard, but let's assume your name really is Bob.

You're sat at your PC starting to put together your CV, when a curious thing happens. You bash out your name on the keyboard and what flickers on the screen? Not Bob, but Robert, Bob's very earliest incarnation. What's going on?

When we put things in writing, we have a tendency to adopt a kind of quasi-formal language that has little connection with our normal lives, but which represents a self-imposed obligation to conform to an imagined literary etiquette. Does it really matter whether you label yourself Bob or Robert on your CV? Is this just pedantic nit-picking? Well, let's roll the story on.

Here's an idea for you...

Check the dates that you cite throughout your CV. (You've done that already? Check them again just to make sure.) It's all too easy to mistype a number and give the impression that there was a gap in your career when there wasn't or that two roles appeared to overlap when they didn't.

You've sent your CV in and you've secured an interview. Cut to the day of your interview and you're sat in the company's reception area waiting to be seen. The person who's about to interview you emerges from the interview room, having checked which candidate is due next, and then heads down to fetch you. As you're the only person in the waiting area, the interviewer strides confidently towards you. You stand up. The interviewer speaks:

Interviewer: Hello, you must be Robert.
Bob: Actually, it's Bob.

Remember that cliché about how you never get a chance to make a second impression? Remember that when we meet people for the first time, we form a view of them within seconds or even less? Well, both statements are true. So, how have you managed that vital first encounter with the interviewer? They've called you Robert and you've corrected them. That's right – your imaginary first exchange has revolved around you telling the interviewer that at some level they've got it wrong. Only it wasn't actually them who got it wrong, as it was you who gave them a piece of duff information.

There's a wider point here. Anything that you put in your CV is liable to be quoted back at you when you have an interview. So, be sure that every item of information you give is accurate.

One of the areas where it's tempting to ever so slightly obfuscate is if your employer has made you redundant. Sometimes the terms of a redundancy include a period of garden leave

There's more on how to manage interviews in IDEA 46, *Handling interviews.*

Try another idea...

such that you're technically on the company's books when you are in fact free to circulate your CV. There's a tendency for people in that position to present themselves as gainfully employed without referring to the imminent departure. Part of the psychology behind that is a belief in that piece of folk wisdom that it's easier to find a job from a job, yet there's actually no substantive evidence to back up that belief.

The problem with doing this will become apparent should you be called to interview. We all know that one of the standard interview questions asks why we've applied for a particular vacancy or why we're looking to move on from our current employer. I've sat in on interviews where a line manager is visibly perturbed to be told by a candidate that they're leaving due to redundancy. It's not actually the redundancy that's perturbed them (most line managers appreciate that redundancy is commonplace these days), it's because there was no hint of it on the CV.

The golden rule is therefore to make sure that there's no aspect of your CV that might cause a conversational hiccough at an interview. By all means impress and dazzle the interviewer with your experience and your personality, just avoid inducing states of momentary confusion by ever so slightly wrong-footing their expectations.

'When a teacher calls a boy by his entire name, it means trouble.'
MARK TWAIN

Defining idea...

How did
it go?

Q **I was brought up on the basis that you used your formal name in formal settings. So, although my friends call me Angie, I feel I should put Angela on my CV. Is this a bad idea?**

A *If you want to call yourself Angela, that's fine. There are no absolute rights and wrongs here. Just be sure to stick to your choice of name throughout the selection process.*

Q **Do you think you might be going a bit over the top on this one?**

A *You might think this is being a bit oversensitive and that one micro-exchange can't really be that significant. However, the point is that you don't want an interview to get off on the wrong foot. If that happens, you might find you can't recover and that the interview goes into a downward spiral. In my book, that's a pretty culpable outcome when you have it within your control to prevent it from happening.*

Q **OK, a quick question about redundancy if I may. I have a job currently, but left the last one due to redundancy. It still upsets me to talk about it, as I believe I was unfairly treated. Can I gloss over the fact on my CV to reduce the chance of the topic coming up?**

A *You don't necessarily have to spell it out on your CV. You can choose not to state a reason for leaving that role. What you shouldn't do is give a false reason, such as implying that you left voluntarily when you clearly didn't. Of course, you may well find that a thorough recruiter will ask you about it anyway.*

28

I'm keen on ping-pong, playing the ukulele and going to the theatre

Do personal interests impress recruiters? They can do, particularly if you think carefully about the mix you choose to outline.

The vast majority of recruiters and career advisers are pretty much in agreement about what constitutes a good CV: comprehensive contact details, a profile statement, lots of examples of personal impact, reverse chronology, typically no more than two A4 sides, keywords and no jargon or acronyms.

Here's an idea for you...

As an alternative to a separate section on your personal hobbies and interests, consider going for a section called, say, 'Other information' and include hobbies and interests alongside things like your date of birth and driving status.

Funnily enough, the area that seems to divide opinions most is the seemingly innocuous personal hobbies and interests section. The crucial question is whether including details of personal leisure activities and interests is liable to boost or reduce the impact of a CV.

In one corner are those recruiters who believe that a section on personal interests gives CV writers an opportunity to provide a more rounded version of themselves. They see it as our chance to show that there's more to us than merely being a corporate workhorse.

In the other corner, you'll find those who think that any suggestion of a life beyond work is at best a distraction and at worst a strong reason for the recruiting organisation to doubt whether they'd get their pound of flesh. After all, somebody who, for example, spends their weekends and evenings pursuing a sporting interest and who also serves on the parents' association of their children's school may not automatically be at the beck and call of their employer.

In my opinion, and I have to stress it is only an opinion (I've not been able to track down any reliable research to conclusively point one way or the other), I'd recommend that you do include some personal interests information. I've worked in two blue-chip companies in recruitment roles and have handled a lot of recruitment assignments and I've never come across a situation where a candidate who sets out their personal interests has suffered as a result. (I suppose theoretically if you mentioned that you did a lot of fundraising for a research laboratory that boasted the world's largest number of smoking beagles, then your application to be director of an animal rights organisation may find itself on shaky ground. But it stretches the credulity that anybody would be foolish enough to include an interest that suggests a lack of empathy with the goals and aims of the organisation they've applied to.)

Your interests are a component of your personal brand. You can find more on how to cultivate this in IDEA 49, *Manage the brand called You*.

Try another idea...

On the other hand, I've witnessed several instances where an applicant has mentioned a hobby or interest that coincidentally is shared by the person recruiting and where that common interest is enough to shift the applicant's CV from the 'not sure' pile to the 'to be interviewed' pile.

The secret when describing your interests is not to go overboard. Mention a dozen outside interests and the recruiting company might legitimately wonder whether you'd have the energy to turn up at work each day. Mention three or four and you suggest that you're a rounded individual.

Within those three or four, you should try to give an example of each of the following:

1. A physical activity – to suggest a good level of personal fitness and health.

2. A mental activity – to show that you have brains to go with brawn.

3. A team-based or cooperative activity – to show that you're not some kind of bunny-boiling psycho-loner and that you can mix with other people.

'Develop interest in life as you see it; in people, things, literature, music – the world is so rich, simply throbbing with rich treasures, beautiful souls and interesting people.'
HENRY MILLER

Defining idea...

137

How did
it go? **Q I can't stand the thought of revealing personal information to a complete stranger. Isn't this information irrelevant in terms of my ability to do the job?**

A *Technically. Unless there are specific allowed criteria for the advertised job, such as bunny girls needing to be female, you don't have to include personal details such as your date of birth, sex, nationality, interests, marital status or whether or not you have children. The key issue, however, isn't so much whether or not you choose to provide this sort of data, but more whether recruiters are likely to be ill disposed to candidates who choose not to. Since the basis on which we're selected for interview or rejected is shrouded in as much mystery as a papal election, it's very hard to get hold of solid information in this respect.*

Q So, should I keep my personal data to myself or not?

A *Personally, I tend to be a pragmatist in this terrain and provide most personal data. I suppose I'm hitting a point in my life where age discrimination might rear its wrinkled head, but I figure that any recruiter worth their salt should be able to work out my age to within a year or two from the information given in my CV such as schooling details. Besides, most personal data isn't really that personal. It's not like employers want details of our bowel movements or how often we have sex.*

29

Set the right tone

OK, so you want to get noticed but you also want that interview so don't want to go over the top in terms of wackiness. Here's what you need to know...

Getting the tone and style right requires a fine balance between presenting your case conservatively and being just that little bit different in order to catch the reader's eye.

The job marketplace has an overwhelmingly conservative outlook. You may come across the occasional recruitment consultant whose palate is jaded through seeing too many CVs and who will advise you that doing something radically different with yours is an important way of distinguishing yourself from the pack. But for every iconoclast like that, you'll find a hundred other recruitment consultants who will tell you that playing it safe is the best strategy.

This is not terribly exciting advice, but for the vast majority of jobs it's counterproductive to do anything more radical that substituting two sheets of white A4 with two sheets of cream A4. To do anything more extreme is simply to create 'noise' around your CV that's more likely to distract than attract.

Unleash your creative streak and put together a CV that has as many wacky features as you can stomach. Then compare it with your 'normal' CV. Which version would you honestly prefer to have circulating in the job marketplace? Can you draw anything at all from the wacky version that would improve the positive impact of your usual version?

So, here are a few dos and don'ts in terms of how to present your CV to the job market:

DON'T send a photo

What is enclosing a photograph intended to achieve anyway? That you're young and virile and have your own head of hair? That your brow is furrowed with the wisdom of years? That you have a natty dress sense? No, the fact is that recruiters don't like photos and in these politically correct times it's not palatable to imply that how you look should have some kind of bearing on whether or not you're interviewed.

DON'T use humour

There are few better ways of bonding with somebody than through a joke shared. But be warned. It's one thing to crack a funny in a convivial setting with a bunch of mates when the drink has been flowing freely; it's another thing entirely to insert something 'amusing' into your CV and then for your CV to turn up under the nose of a complete stranger who may be having a rotten day and who may not share your sense of humour. Don't risk it.

DON'T mess with people's expectations

Recruiters expect to see a CV set out in a standard format, using a sensible font. Any attempt on your part to subvert those expectations is more likely to rebound on you than anything else.

DO match the CV to the job you're going for

Most job applications benefit from a fairly conservative approach. The only exceptions are for jobs where a talent for innovation or creativity is explicitly required by the jobholder. In those rare cases, trying something a little bolder or more outlandish might bring home the bacon.

If you're in the mood for more 'don't do' stuff, brace yourself for IDEA 17, *The seven deadly CV sins.*

Try another idea...

DO dress conservatively

If your CV secures you an interview, make an effort to turn up looking well presented. If you turn up for an interview wearing clothes that fitted you perfectly in the pre-paunch 1980s, with evidence of that morning's breakfast mingling with your ZZ Top beard, not to mention whiffing gently of last night's garlic bread and sporting a hairstyle borrowed from Tom Hanks in the latter stages of *Castaway*, you can pretty much kiss that job goodbye.

'*If you're thinking of finding a new job, it's worth knowing that only 7% of those recruiting staff look favourably on CVs with quirky features such as photos or humour. So play it straight.*'
JULIA FEUELL, Managing Director of New Frontiers

Defining idea...

Q **I can't decide whether my CV needs to be more eye-catching or more conservative. Do you have any tips?**

A *You've put your finger on the great CV paradox. How can your CV stand out from the competition without standing out so much that employers will get nervous about you? Actually, there is no paradox really: if you want to stand out in a crowd, by all means don a clown's outfit; if you want your CV to stand out in a recruiter's eyes, concentrate on professional, well-presented content rather than coloured paper and presentational gimmickry.*

Q **Actually, I consider myself a bit of a character. In fact, people tell me I'm larger than life. Shouldn't that come through in my CV?**

A *It's your choice of course. At one level I'm all for being authentic when it comes to CVs. If we sat in a bath of cold beans for charity a couple of years ago, why shouldn't the recruitment world know? If we send all our personal correspondence out accompanied by tiny glittery stars that scatter all over the floor when the envelope is opened, why shackle our style when we apply for jobs? Unfortunately, employers tend to respond to conservatism in a CV, not flamboyance, and the plain facts are that 'characterful' CVs have a lower success rate in terms of interview invitations than their 'does what it says on the tin' counterparts. Reflect your outrageous self in your CV by all means, but be aware that as a direct consequence you'll likely have to wait a while for an employer to come along who is prepared to take on the full-on, unexpurgated, bean-dripping you.*

30

Apply yourself

Always popular in the public and voluntary sectors, private companies are increasingly using application forms as a way of acquiring behavioural information about candidates.

For the job-hunter, application forms are a pain in the butt. You spend hours honing and refining your CV so that it makes your optimal business case for an interview only to find that your next potential employer isn't interested in seeing it.

However, from the point of view of many recruiters, advertisements that invite CVs these days are more likely to attract too many applications. In contrast, advertisements that ask for an application form to be completed typically have a lower response rate. So, from an organisation's perspective application forms can be a nifty way to reduce the time and money spent on the vacancy-filling process.

There's a shadow side to this, of course, namely that fewer applicants can mean a lower quality field. This means that if you can face the prospect of completing an application form without losing the will to live, you'll find that you'll typically be up against a smaller field of competition.

Here's an idea for you...

Complete the application form fully and don't skimp on the detail. And although it might be tempting simply to send your CV with the form, with 'See my CV' written in as many sections as possible, you'll come over as both lazy and disinterested.

Here are some reasons why organisations like application forms:

1. Application forms ask all candidates for the same information and are regarded by the Advisory, Conciliation and Arbitration Service *et al.* as good equal opportunities practice.

2. They allow the company to specify the information that applicants need to provide.

3. They allow a readier comparison between candidates because every candidate is completing the same form. Not literally the same form – that would be an administrative nightmare obviously!

TIPS ON COMPLETING APPLICATION FORMS

1. Unless you have the drafting skills of a Benedictine monk, it makes sense to take a photocopy of the form so that you can draft out a rough version first. Multiple crossings out and handwriting that becomes increasingly smaller as you desperately try to squeeze your doubtless brilliant prose into a tiny space on the form are great ways to demonstrate that you're as human as the rest of us, but they don't go down a bundle with the personnel department.

2. Use a black or dark blue pen – light turquoise ink may hint at your creative side, but it's a bugger to read and just as bad to photocopy.

3. Ask yourself what the recruiting organisation is looking for in the right candidate. Then tailor the information you provide accordingly.

Received an application form that wants you to give lots of behavioural examples? Check out IDEA 10, *Learn to speak 'behaviourese'*, for a crash course.

Try another idea...

4. Answer the questions as fully as possible, but don't waffle. Show that you can organise and express your thoughts clearly.

5. There's normally a section of the application form that gives you an opportunity to make a personal statement. Use every last inch of it (and continue on a separate sheet if you need to). This might be your least favourite part of an application form, and it will almost certainly take the longest to complete, but it's a major opportunity to distinguish yourself from the competition. Highlight some relevant achievements and show that you've taken the time to find out something about the company ('Given your recently announced plans to launch a new product...').

6. Before popping the original in the post, remember to take a copy for yourself.

7. Knock up a short covering letter to go with the application form. Remember to quote the reference number and say where you saw the advert.

8. Go to the post office and splash out on some A4 envelopes so that the application turns up uncrumpled at the other end. Alternatively, liberate a few from the office stationery cupboard.

'Perseverance is a great element of success. If you only knock long enough and loud enough at the gate, you are sure to wake somebody.'
HENRY WADSWORTH LONGFELLOW

Defining idea...

How did it go?

Q I've just received an application pack for a job I fancy, but the blighters want me to fill in their application form. Can't I just send them my CV instead?

A *You can, but don't expect an invitation to interview! Organisations that choose to use application forms as a basis for recruitment rather than CVs expect applicants to conform to their chosen approach. Barring exceptional circumstances, such as an incredibly low response, candidates who send a CV and don't complete the application form will be rejected.*

Q But don't you find that filling out application forms is extremely time-consuming? I'd rather spend my days at the gym than filling out poxy paperwork.

A *That's partly the point. Employers are savvy enough to know that using application forms will inhibit response rates. They figure that the people who can't be bothered to fill in their forms are unlikely to be the best recruitment catches. Let's face it, it doesn't say much for your motivation if an hour or two providing information to an employer's specification is beyond you.*

Q I've decided to fill out the application form after all. There's not much space allocated to some parts and I'm finding it difficult to get over all the information I consider relevant. Is it OK to attach a copy of my CV in those circumstances?

A *Check the paperwork from the organisation to see if they have a stance on CVs. Unless there's a note somewhere saying that CVs are expressly not wanted, go ahead. On your point about the size of some of the boxes on an application form, if you can't fit in all of the information you want to, continue on a separate sheet.*

31

Surfing CVs

A reminder that job searching has gone digital.

Those of you in your forties or fifties with a disdain for new technology had better be warned that there's a generation of internet-savvy, technologically hip people coming through who may well turn out to be the reason why you don't get your next promotion or job offer.

It's reckoned that anything up to 80% of medium to large organisations use some form of electronic scanning system to process CVs. Additionally, there are a growing number of smaller companies that buy in recruitment services from external providers who in turn make use of scanning systems. Top that up with the huge growth in online recruitment services and you've got a significant portion of the recruitment market where the first sift and cut of CVs is put together by an unfeeling machine as opposed to somebody from Personnel (apparently, there's a difference between the two).

Here's an idea for you... **Use both general and specific keywords. For example, if the recruiting organisation is looking for somebody who is comfortable using standard business software packages, it's worthwhile listing both Microsoft Office as a generic name and the specific programmes like Microsoft Word, Excel, PowerPoint, and so on.**

HOW ELECTRONIC SCANNING WORKS

Think of electronic scanning as a three-step process:

Step 1 On arrival, a CV is fed through a scanner and then converted into a 'readable' file.

Step 2 The computer rummages through the file for keywords (i.e. relevant skills, experience, knowledge, abilities and education) and places the CV in an appropriate database.

Step 3 When a vacancy arises, the employer uses an applicant tracking system to locate and extract the CVs that contain the keywords associated with the role being filled.

This matching process works effectively when matching people with 'hard' skills and so the individuals who are popular on databases are people in professions like engineering, computer science, finance, accounting, marketing, management and human resources. Anybody working in 'softer' areas like fashion design or the visual arts may find that their experience doesn't suit this medium.

TACTICS FOR SURVIVING THE CUT

How does the fact that a significant chunk of the recruitment market now uses electronic CV databases to search for people with specific experience and qualifications impact on the way in which we put our CVs together?

Well, the most important thing is to make sure that we include the right keywords in our CV. For this reason, it's best to describe our experience with concrete words rather than vague descriptions.

To ensure that your CV goes through a scanner as productively as possible, remember the following:

1. Use white A4 paper for best results; definitely avoid tinted paper as this can significantly undermine the scanner's character-reading capability.

2. Print on one side only.

3. Provide a laser-printed original for the best results. A typewritten original or a high-quality photocopy are also OK. Avoid dot-matrix printouts (you still have a dot-matrix printer...?) and low-quality photocopies.

4. Don't fold or staple the pages.

Don't rely on the internet alone as a job-finding strategy. Get out and meet some people too, but before you go have a look at IDEA 45, *Dealing with specialist recruiters*.

Try another idea...

149

5. Use standard typefaces. Avoid fancy styles such as italics, underline, shadows and reverses (white letters on black background). Definitely avoid typefaces where the letters touch each other as character-reading software really struggles to interpret this.

6. Use a font size of no less than ten points and no bigger than fourteen points.

7. Avoid gimmicks like a two-column format or presenting your CV in the form of a newspaper or newsletter.

You need to ensure that your CV looks the part for both electronic and human scanning. There are still plenty of organisations where electronic scanning isn't used and so you need to cover all the angles. In other words, you need to use keywords in your CV while also ensuring that it still looks easy on the eye.

Oh, and one final point. Electronic scanning is another reason why you really must make sure that you avoid typos. For example, if 'Excel' is a keyword and you've spelt it 'Exsel', then the vast majority of scanning systems would have you logged as somebody with no Excel experience.

Defining idea...

'The medium is the message.'
MARSHALL MCLUHAN

Q **I've had a go at including keywords. My CV looks OK, but how can I be sure that I have the right keywords?**

How did it go?

A *You're right to be concerned. Coming up with the right keywords is a must. The secret is to be as concrete and specific as possible with your language. The good news is that electronic scanning systems don't penalise you for including too many keywords, only for failing to identify the right ones. For that reason, feel uninhibited about including terms that you feel just might be relevant. Remember as well that if the original advertisement has done its job, most of the relevant keywords shouldn't be that hard to identify.*

Q **How can I include all the keywords I want without making my CV look messy and cluttered to the human eye?**

A *That's fairly straightforward. Include as many keywords as you can in the natural flow of the CV and then put the rest in a section named 'Keywords' and your CV will still look aesthetically OK.*

32

Transatlantic issues

CVs that work here won't necessarily work elsewhere. Be sure to arm yourself with a pond-crossing, stateside stunner of a résumé.

George Bernard Shaw's observation that the US and the UK are 'two nations divided by a common language' still holds good today. Don't let a shared core of vocabulary fool you into thinking that you know what your transatlantic business chums are talking about!

For example, to 'table' a motion in a British boardroom will see it discussed. In America, 'tabling' something will see it put firmly on the back burner. Anybody planning to apply for a job in the US will need to be alert to these types of shifts in meaning, but converting a CV into an American-style résumé requires more than just a bit of attention to vocabulary.

Don't mention your gender, race, religion or marital status unless it's appropriate and relevant for the job. In most American states, employers are under a legal obligation to be fair and not to discriminate against applicants because of their gender, race or sexual orientation.

Although there are some similarities between the way that CVs and résumés are put together, there are also a number of subtle and not so subtle distinctions. A typical US résumé begins by listing contact details (don't include a heading that says 'Résumé'). It then goes into some if not all of the following sections:

- Objective
- Executive profile
- Professional experience
- Credentials/education
- Languages
- Computer skills
- Personal information

To take each section in turn:

Objective

Most US career experts recommend including this section. It comes just below your contact information and sets out in two or three lines what you're shooting for in terms of your next career move. Here's an example: 'Senior Executive position where a proven record of achievement through leadership, team building and strategic thinking will maximise the financial and corporate goals.'

Executive profile

Most US career experts believe that an executive profile serves a positive purpose. US profiles tend to run a bit longer than their European counterparts – ten to twelve lines isn't uncommon.

Want to find a job in America but don't live there? Now's a good time to look at IDEA 31, *Surfing CVs*, for a few pointers on how the internet might be able to help you.

Try another idea...

It can work quite well to devote the first chunk of the profile to breadth of experience and responsibilities and then go on to a sub-section called something like Personal Qualities, which features a few lines of 'High energy, flexible, take charge executive with a strong reputation for integrity' type stuff.

Professional experience

As in Europe, the reverse chronology model is more popular than the functional. Whichever format you opt for, look to fill your work experience with keywords that highlight your experience to date and your skills. Electronic scanning of CVs is more popular in the US. Be sure to include details of the post that your role reports to.

Credentials/education

Credentials: This covers professional qualifications and details of degrees and post-graduate qualifications, set out in reverse chronology order. Any long or prestigious courses, such as spells at Harvard or London Business School, are also worth mentioning.

'If you can speak three languages you're trilingual. If you can speak two languages you're bilingual. If you can speak only one language you're an American.'
ANONYMOUS

Defining idea...

Education: This section should come before the one on professional experience if you're in school or have been out of school for only a couple of years, depending on your level of work experience and how relevant your education is to your career.

Languages (optional)
If relevant to the job, list the languages you speak and your level of competence, i.e. whether you can translate, speak or write in each language and how well.

Computer skills (optional)
List the programmes, applications, etc., that you can use and your level of competence.

Personal information (optional)
Consider including a brief section where you can list personal information such as hobbies or interests as this can add value. Be very succinct, i.e. no more than three or four words per item.

Attachments
Always attach a cover letter with the résumé, but don't send diplomas or documents unless specifically asked to. Don't send a photo unless it's relevant to the job, such as modelling or acting.

Q **I've had a go at putting together a CV aimed at the American market. I'm fairly happy with it, but how can I tell if I'm pushing the right buttons?**

How did it go?

A *There are a number of ways that you can test this. First, have a look at a number of US recruitment websites, which will give you information about putting a résumé together. You should also find some sample résumés, which will provide some concrete pointers on current résumé fashions. The real key is to get some feedback from people who understand the US job market. Try emailing a copy of your résumé to US recruitment companies and specifically seek feedback on how well you've pitched your proposition.*

Q **I've emailed some US recruitment agencies for feedback as you suggested, but I've heard nothing. Any suggestions?**

A *To be honest, using the internet can be a bit hit and miss so you may not get any replies. As an alternative, drop into an employment agency in the UK that has outlets in the US, tell them what you're looking to achieve and ask to plug into their international placement operation. You can then use your charm and persuasion to request some feedback from somebody in their US division – this is a lot more likely to happen now that you're a known face and an active client of theirs.*

33
Please find attached...

A top-notch covering letter can be viewed as either essential or totally unnecessary and we've no way of knowing which is the case.

Before the advent of the personal computer, say, twenty years ago, the content of your CV could almost have been carved in stone. Once composed, it would have rarely changed, regardless of where it was being sent.

This was because much more emphasis used to be put on the covering letter, which was then *de rigueur*. Your CV would simply have described your career to date in fairly neutral terms. Your covering letter was supposed to map out why you were the perfect person to fill the vacancy.

So, in effect, the accompanying letter was the 'one-to-one marketing document' that the CV has now become. But because we now adapt and alter our CVs virtually every time we send them out to potential employers, a huge question mark hangs over the covering letter. In terms of how the covering letter is regarded nowadays, there are two distinct camps in the recruiters' world.

Here's an idea for you...

Always find a named person to write to. Anything addressed to 'The Personnel Manager' or opening with 'Dear Sir/Madam' is liable to end up on the desk of an admin underling. If, on the other hand, you write to an individual personally, you'll turn the epistolary equivalent of a cold call into a much warmer approach.

In one camp are those recruiters who bin accompanying letters on sight because they expect applicants to make their case entirely through their CV. They assume that people will produce a customised CV and that therefore an accompanying letter is simply a lingering nod to a piece of outmoded social etiquette. Spend forty minutes carefully crafting a bespoke letter in these cases and it'll be a waste of time as its unlikely to make any difference to the recruiter's decision about whether or not you deserve an interview.

In the second camp, there are just as many recruiters who expect to see a covering letter that sets out a full and convincing argument why the writer should be pencilled in for an interview. In these cases, the absence of a covering letter would do your cause real harm.

The catch is that we rarely know which of these two camps we're likely to be dealing with when popping our details in the post. The safest bet for the prudent job-hunter is to therefore write a covering letter on the basis that it just might make a difference.

Defining idea...

'Everyone lives by selling something.'
ROBERT LOUIS STEVENSON

Your covering letter should obviously be typed, regardless of how neat your handwriting is. No recruiter I know will read a handwritten letter in preference to one that's typed. And regarding the content of a covering letter, the structure can be broken down into three sections:

> **Why not get a second opinion on your covering letter. Go to IDEA 41, *I'll show you mine if you show me yours*, for more on this.**

Try another idea...

1. Make the connection
Explain why you're writing at this particular time. If it's in response to an advertisement, identify where you saw the ad and when it appeared (this can help recruiters to identify which papers or magazines bring in the best response). If your approach is speculative, still try to give a compelling reason why you're interested in that particular company.

2. Make your pitch
Describe what you can offer the company. Try to make sure that every point you make is likely to be relevant to their needs.

3. Describe what's coming next
Take control of the process by saying what you want to happen next. Perhaps say something like, 'I'll call you in a week's time to see if there might be value in our meeting up' or a less pushy 'I look forward to hearing from you.' Follow up with a telephone call if you've heard nothing after ten days or so.

> *'To be persuasive, we must be believable. To be believable, we must be credible. To be credible, we must be truthful.'*
> HELLMUT WALTERS, German thinker

Defining idea...

How did it go?

Q   I've drafted a covering letter, but I'm not sure if it's any good. Any tips?

A   *If you've followed the three-point approach I've suggested I'm sure you'll have a good basic shape to your letter.*

Q   I'm quite comfortable with making the pitch and setting out what I want to happen next, but can you say a bit more about making the connection?

A   *You're right to focus on your opening gambit. A covering letter that reads like it might have been sent to dozens of other companies will get you nowhere. Instead, put some clear blue water between your approach and the thousands of cold CVs that turn up every day in corporate post rooms the length and breadth of the land. Here are three example openers:*

- *'One of your colleagues, Gordon Ramsay in your catering division, suggested that I drop you a line.'*

- *'I recently read in an article in* The World of Cheese *journal that you're planning to expand your operations into Europe and so I'm writing to see if you have any openings for...'*

- *'I was playing golf with your MD, who suggested I got in touch.'*

34

Bring me the head of Johnny Recruiter

The lowdown on what recruiters say will push their buttons and what will get on their nerves.

A little while back, I organised a get together with some HR chums to extract their views about what constitutes a good CV these days.

Now, these were people who have seen thousands of CVs in their time, 98% of which don't make the cut. So, their opinions should count for something. I asked them two questions:

1. When you're reviewing a CV, what factors will cause you to reject the candidate?

2. What's your advice for anybody who wants to put together a top-notch CV?

I hope the following responses are helpful. If you don't like what you see, then blame it on the HR mindset and not me!

Here's an idea for you...

Ensure that the company research you've carried out comes over in your CV and covering letter. Mention project names, products, site, locations, whatever. If your research doesn't show up explicitly somewhere, you won't get credit for it.

Rejection factors

The main reasons that recruiters give for rejecting a CV are:

- Questionable grammar
- CV doesn't read well
- Spelling mistakes
- CV is overlength
- CV provides too little information
- Applicant is underqualified
- Applicant is overqualified
- An emphasis on skills when the ad stressed achievements
- An emphasis on achievements when the ad stressed skills
- Too much personal information
- Poor choice of font, making CV hard to read
- Too much emphasis on early career
- Lack of evidence to back up claims in the profile
- Too much information on extracurricular activities

It's worth making a point here about the importance of context. If a recruiter has, say, 500 CVs to look at and a target shortlist of ten people to interview plus six to ten reserves, relatively minor transgressions or failings on the part of the applicant can result in a rejection letter.

Where there's a much smaller field of applicants, a degree of pragmatism kicks in with recruiters and the focus is almost entirely on the extent to which applicants meet or don't meet the core specification.

Tips for a top-notch CV

Here are some pretty much verbatim words from the wise about what recruiters see as good CV-writing practice:

1. Make sure that the CV has no grammatical or spelling errors.

2. Try to inject a positive outlook into the CV.

3. Keep the length to two pages ideally, three at the most.

4. For me, content is king. Length isn't important. I've been bored by two-page CVs and fascinated by six-page CVs.

5. Only include details that positively sell you. A CV is a marketing document, not a confession.

6. When it comes to describing your knowledge and experience, don't include any information simply because you feel it ought to go in. Ask yourself whether that piece of information will make it more likely that you'll be called for interview. If you think it will, put it in.

If you're partial to a bit of advice from the sharp end, check out **IDEA 3**, *How long do I have?*, for further views on the length of the ideal CV.

Try another idea...

'*Some problems are so complex that you have to be highly intelligent and well informed just to be undecided about them.*'
LAURENCE J. PETER, author of *The Peter Principle*

Defining idea...

7. Provide evidence to back up any claims. For example, it's all very well talking about having 'exemplary team management skills', but without some kind of evidence to back this up it's just bullshit as far as I'm concerned.

8. Use active verbs to give the CV a bit of oomph. I like to get a sense of energy from the CV.

9. Avoid management speak. Unlike an elephant with a PhD, it's not big and it's not clever.

10. No photos please. We have files for over two thousand employees and I can't think of one person whose CV came with a photo.

11. Avoid gimmicks. Perhaps I'm perverse, but the more somebody tries to catch my eye with anything other than content, the more I'm inclined to reject them.

12. Be explicit about how you match the specification and make it apparent as quickly as possible. Remember that most recruiters barely have the time to read all the lines, let alone between them!

13. Don't repeat yourself. I remember one CV where the same information was replicated word for word in the covering letter, in the career highlights section of the CV and again under the individual job headings. Not only is it a waste of space, but the law of diminishing returns makes three references have a lot less of an impact than just one.

14. I like to see information on hobbies and interests. It humanises the application.

15. A section on hobbies and interests is just dead space in my view. Far better to include some extra work-relevant material.

16. A meaningful covering letter is a must in my book. It shows a higher level of commitment by the applicant and gives them the chance to hit me with their best shots.

Q Are your HR contacts really the best source of advice or should we be listening more to line managers?

How did it go?

A *Funnily enough, I had a conversation about CVs with a group of line managers a couple of years ago. There's actually very little difference in outlook between the two groups. The only distinction I can recall is that these particular line managers were even less tolerant of gimmicks than their HR counterparts and had no time for the likes of photos, use of colour, non-standard paper or management speak.*

Q What general conclusions can be drawn from the views that your HR contacts have expressed?

A *You no doubt noticed that some of the advice is contradictory. When all is said and done, what we're discussing here is an H2H (human to human) communication process. Even the most professional recruiters have their foibles. Mind you, so do line managers. I remember that a particular line manager I interviewed with on a number of occasions would drop his pencil on the floor during the course of an interview so that he could check out the state of the interviewee's shoes. He maintained that highly polished shoes predicted a highly polished performance on the job!*

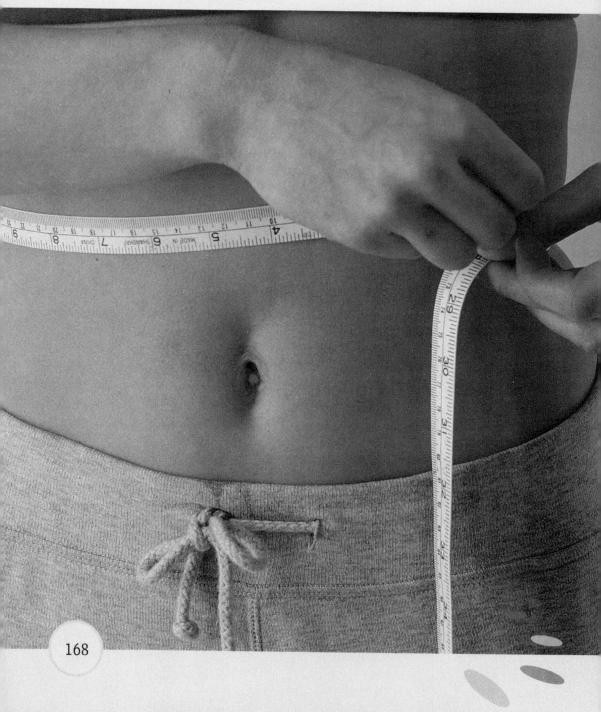

35

Time to shed some pounds?

Avoid giving details of your salary in your CV. If you're specifically asked to do so, however, here are some tips on how to go about it.

In a perfect job-hunting world, your current salary will nuzzle a perfect thousand or two below the starting salary outlined in the advertisement for your next potential post.

But how do you play things if you either earn a lot more or a lot less than the stated salary range in an advertisement you're keen to respond to and you're asked to give details of your current salary?

This situation can easily arise. Perhaps you earn a fortune in your current job and don't want to price yourself out of the market. Or maybe you have a bit of a pension coming in and therefore don't need to maintain your current salary level. Or your current company is in a notoriously low-paying sector.

DON'T SHOW THEM THE MONEY

In my opinion, a direct answer to the salary question will hurt your chances. Think about it. A typical job advertisement in something like the UK's *Sunday Times* can

If you feel that your new employer might struggle to match your current salary, develop a package of non-salary elements that could form an alternative negotiating package. Such elements could include flexible working, holiday entitlement, education assistance, car, laptop, professional organisation membership, gym fees, health insurance and severance package.

generate literally hundreds of CVs. One of the easier ways in which that poor sod in the personnel department can whittle down numbers is to weed out any applicants who are too expensive and therefore quite possibly overqualified. The same goes for applicants whose salaries are too low, implying that that they might be underqualified.

Though it's tempting to do so, don't simply ignore the request for salary information. If the advertisement specifically requests a response, not providing one will have you labelled by the recruiter as either rude (because you didn't bother to respond) or someone with poor attention to detail (because you didn't notice the reference to salary information). Neither of those labels is going to have you waltzing into an interview.

Consider including one of the following explanations in your covering letter (you should always keep salary information away from your CV):

- 'My salary requirements are negotiable.'
- 'My salary history is consistent with my experience and record of achievements.'
- 'My salary consists of a number of elements, including a performance-related payment. I will be happy to talk these through in more detail at a meeting.'

By giving some kind of response, you've shown that you've read the ad, even if you're choosing to evade the issue. Most recruitment consultants and HR managers that I know tell me that they wouldn't take offence at any of the responses above. Actually, one HR contact told me that any of those replies would give them one less reason not to call the applicant.

Salary isn't the only area where you can scupper your chances of getting an interview if you play it wrong. Check out IDEA 39, *Detox your CV.*

Try another idea...

TALKING SALARY FACE-TO-FACE

If your response on salary has satisfied the recruiter and they like the look of your experience and qualifications, there's more than a fighting chance that you'll get an interview. Having bought yourself a bit of time in terms of the salary question, you can think about how to play things when you're face-to-face with the interviewer.

First things first. If the interviewer doesn't raise the subject of salary, then you shouldn't either. Presenting yourself at interview is a sales process, whereas talking salary is a negotiation process. Trying to sell yourself and negotiate simultaneously weakens your bargaining hand. Sell yourself at interview and subsequently get a job offer, then you've got a very strong buying signal from the company and you can negotiate from a position of real strength.

However, if the question of the salary you require does arise, you can try saying that you'd like to make as much as other employees with your qualifications. Or you could try answering the question with a question like 'What is a typical salary for this position?' Another alternative is to respond by giving a pay range rather than a specific figure.

'Why is there so much month left at the end of the money?'
JOHN BARRYMORE, actor

Defining idea...

171

And if you're pressed to give details of your current salary, you have a number of options. If you're trying to play down your current rate then consider simply giving them your basic salary. If you need to increase the value of your package then you could give a number that encapsulates everything down to the luncheon vouchers.

How did it go?

Q **I've found my perfect next job. It pays quite a bit less than I'm currently on, but I've got a bit of a pension and a few bob coming in from investments so I can afford the drop. Any further tips regarding how I should play things?**

A *If they expressly ask what you're currently on, give them the absolute basic rate. If that's still too high, you can add that your previous company was noted for paying well above the market rate. You could also pitch the line that the salary offered is only one consideration in taking a position – opportunities for personal and career development, to cut down commuting time or maybe work flexible hours are just as important.*

Q **What if my perfect job didn't turn out to be so perfect after all and I wanted to look for a job at my former higher salary. How would I play the salary question then?**

A *There's no foolproof way out of this one. I'd recommend telling them openly that you took a job that didn't pan out and that the experience has confirmed to you that your former work was what you really love and what you're really best at. Then cross your fingers and hope that your previous track record is good enough to outweigh this slight career aberration.*

36

Reference points

I'm sure you can rustle up two people who would write something vaguely complimentary about you. Even so, manage the process, don't leave it to chance.

The South African golfer Gary Player was once asked whether he thought he was lucky on the golf course. 'Yes', he reportedly answered, 'and the more I practise the luckier I get.'

There's a clear message here for all aspiring job-changers: to get the best results, leave as little to chance as possible. For most of the process of putting a CV together, control is very much in our own hands. We choose the format, determine the content and style, and decide who to send it to.

Typically, though, when it comes to providing the names of referees to potential employers, we can find ourselves resorting to giving the contact details of a complete stranger, all too often a no-name jobsworth in the personnel department.

Make it clear to colleagues past and present that you're very happy to provide a reference for them. This will both earn you their gratitude and help you to keep tabs on who is moving where. In so doing you'll provide yourself with a range of networking contacts in different organisations.

But is this really the best person you can come up with to impress the next prospective payer of your salary? Possibly not. Unless that person knows you personally, chances are they'll pass the reference request to one of their admin team who will dig out your file from the archives during a quiet moment. Apart from confirming the dates you worked for the company and maybe providing details of your sick record while employed there, the best you're likely to get out of that administrator is a bland, non-committal 'know of no reason why the candidate should not be taken on' reference. Not damaging admittedly, but no glowing testimonial either. So, how can we sort the referential wheat from the chaff?

According to the UK Chartered Institute of Personnel and Development, most potential employers still make a point of seeking written references before confirming a job offer. Therefore, it's worth putting a bit of care into identifying people who are well placed to comment positively on you and the contribution you have made. Ideally, have a range of possible referees on the stocks so that you can put the most appropriate set of names up to the company that wants to take you on.

Defining idea...

'I can live for two months on a good compliment.'
MARK TWAIN

What will clinch a good reference for you, though, isn't so much the people you choose, but how well you manage your dealings with those individuals. I've had requests for references pop through the letterbox from time to time for people who I've worked with or known in the past.

There's more on developing contacts in IDEA 43, Networking.

Try another idea...

Call me Mr Grumpy if you like, but I object to these requests just turning up out of the blue. In my mind, there's a certain etiquette to be followed here. Before naming anybody as a referee, I'd recommend making contact with them to ensure that they're happy to provide a reference. And remember that although the details of your spells working with that individual may be etched in your brain, your referee may well not remember your precise job title, the dates that you worked with them or indeed some of your specific achievements. For that reason, it makes good sense to let them have a copy of your CV so that they can refresh their memory.

Depending on the relationship you have with your referee, you might even want to supply a draft reference that they might care to use. This way, you can be assured of a positive write-up. You've also re-established a connection with somebody who might well be a very useful networking contact at some point in the future.

'If you want to win friends, make it a point to remember them. If you remember my name, you pay me a subtle compliment; you indicate that I have made an impression on you. Remember my name and you add to my feeling of importance.'
DALE CARNEGIE

Defining idea...

How did
it go?

Q **I supplied references to my new employer some time ago, but I spoke last night to one of the people I named as a referee and they've heard nothing. What should I do?**

A *Unless you're the new HR Director, nothing! It's the employer's responsibility to take up references. If they choose not to do so or forget to ask, then it's not your problem. If you are the new HR Director, then it's time to put a rocket under your recruitment people and remind them that references are one of the primary tools available to the organisation to find out if candidates have told the truth about themselves.*

Q **I've been told that my last employer refuses to supply references for any of their employees. Can that be right?**

A *Yes, an employer can refuse to provide a reference. There is no statutory duty to provide an existing employee or ex-employee with a reference. The vast majority of employers, however, will supply references on request from a legitimate source.*

Q **I supplied details of a personal referee, but I've been told that this isn't acceptable. Is this normal?**

A *References are usually sought from current and former employers. Some companies take the view that information from personal referees is of low value. For example, British Telecom don't take up personal references for graduate recruitment, as they're always complimentary!*

37

Is it convenient to talk?

Life can be cruel. Shortlisted candidates can be demoted to the reserve list if they cannot be reached by phone for whatever reason.

If your CV fits the bill, recruiters will want to get hold of you and you'll need to be able to answer their call professionally no matter where and when it comes.

Picture this. A line manager picks out half a dozen applicants for interview, gives the personnel department a date for the interviews to take place and asks them to get at least four candidates in. The personnel assistant then gets on the phone and starts ringing around. One candidate's home phone number rings and rings. There's no mobile number on the CV so the assistant puts that candidate's details to one side and then moves on to the next name on the list. Maybe the candidate had simply popped down to the local shops to buy a paper; whatever the reason, they'll now only get a call if none of the four candidates called in for interview are up to scratch.

The first moral of the story is to get an answerphone for the home line. Second, get a mobile. Third, make sure that you list your mobile number on your CV.

Always have a copy of your CV, the job advertisement and any notes you may have made about the job to hand by the home phone. If you think you might be called on your mobile, consider taking the paperwork with you when you leave the house.

If you think that I'm exaggerating the random and whimsical nature of fate, a recruiter told me last week that I'd actually overstated things a bit. He told me that these days he doesn't even bother to ring the home number.

SCREENING INTERVIEWS

Aside from fixing an interview, the telephone plays another key part in the job-hunting process, as many companies now carry out an initial screening of candidates by phone. What this means for us is that the phone could ring at just about any time of the day or evening with a recruiter on the other end of the line hoping to talk with us. If they've called at a deeply inconvenient moment (the washing machine has flooded the kitchen, the dog's thrown up on duvet, siblings are bashing chunks out of each other, etc.) then don't try to field the call. There are no points given by recruiters for stoicism in the face of domestic chaos. It's far better to arrange a different time for the conversation.

When the time comes for the conversation to happen, you need to make sure that you have somewhere quiet where you can hold a decent conversation. If you can't guarantee the requisite level of tranquillity in the area where your phone is sited, you might want to think about using the extension in the

Defining idea... **'The most important thing in communication is to hear what isn't being said.'**
PETER DRUCKER, management guru

bedroom. Alternatively, get hold of a portable phone so that you can head off to the most conducive room available.

If you want to work on getting your message across succinctly, check out IDEA 44, *Perfect your personal elevator pitch.*

Try another idea...

MOBILE PHONE ETIQUETTE

Taking a call on your mobile from a recruiter also needs a bit of careful handling. Remember, don't field the call unless the conditions are right. The mobile has spawned a new breed of very public private conversations. These days it seems that you can't get off at the end of a train journey without knowing rather more than you'd ever want to about a complete stranger's business dealings or (lord preserve us) sexual peccadilloes. But trying to have a sensible conversation with a recruiter in front of all your mates will end in tears.

So, if you receive a call on your mobile at an inconvenient moment, take control of the situation. Not answering is one option. Pavlov's dogs may start dribbling as a conditioned response at the mere ring of a bell, but theoretically we're made of sterner stuff. If you do field the call, however, consider rescheduling it. It's far better to tell the recruiter that you'll ring them back than to shout down the phone that the train you're on is just about to go into a tunnel and that you're going to be cut...

'If I called the wrong number, why did you answer the phone?'
JAMES THURBER

Defining idea...

179

How did it go?

Q   I've yet to experience a telephone interview. How common are they?

A   *Companies are increasingly using telephone interviews. In 2004, The Chartered Institute of Personnel and Development found that 26% of organisations made use of telephone interviews. They are most common in the service sector, with 38% of organisations using them.*

Q   I've just received a letter saying that a company I've applied to will be in touch to conduct a telephone interview. What should I expect?

A   *Telephone interviews take four basic forms:*

1. *A short, highly structured interview aimed specifically at identifying and discounting unsuitable applicants. This is likely to focus on essential criteria from the job's person specification and whether a candidate has the level of qualifications required by the organisation.*

2. *An initial interview using multiple-choice questions to assess a candidate against the required competences.*

3. *An in-depth interview. For senior and managerial positions, this form would be used as a means of selecting candidates for a face-to-face interview shortlist. This method is also used where the organisation is recruiting staff that need to be able to deal well with difficult customers over the telephone. In these cases, role play is sometimes used to assess the candidate's strengths and weaknesses.*

4. *An automated interview in which the initial stage of the recruitment process is fully automated using the telephone keypad.*

38

Bend the facts a little

All organisations develop their own particular language and acronyms, but bear in mind that these may need explaining to an outsider. In fact, it might be better to avoid them altogether.

Have you seen the episode of The Simpsons in which Homer starts an internet business? The job title he initially goes for is 'Chief Executive'. However, he then decides to change it to 'Junior Chief Executive', as he thinks this sounds far more important.

Now although you may not have enough organisational clout to determine what job title you go by in the workplace, it's a different kettle of fish when it comes to your CV. For example, if the job titles you've had over the years don't adequately convey what the jobs were about, feel free to adjust some of the content of your CV to make it more readily comprehensible to recruiters.

Here's an idea for you... **Show your CV to someone who doesn't work for your organisation. Is there anything they couldn't understand?**

The language used in the workplace has always been tempered by historical practice and office politics. There was a story in the papers about four years ago concerning one of the main Whitehall departments that used to run a course called 'Getting the Most Out of Your Junior Staff'. One of the juniors objected to the title and the course was consequently renamed 'Succeeding with Teams'. The content, needless to say, was identical.

CONFUSING JOB TITLES

Now let's be clear about one thing. I'm not advocating gratuitous inflation of the facts in order to make you seem like a bigger organisational hitter than you truly are. For example, it would be plain wrong to call yourself a Project Director when your most important contribution is to fetch everybody coffee. To describe yourself as a Director in those circumstances is to be the type of person that the Texans call all hat and no cattle.

On the other hand, what if your job title is something like Executive Officer (Finance Division)? I'd suggest that this title conveys relatively little about what you actually do. If the reality is that you orchestrate and control most of the company's purchasing from outside suppliers, then calling yourself a Purchasing Manager on your CV is a reasonable translation of your responsibilities into language that would be more meaningful to somebody working in another company.

Defining idea... **'Clutter is the disease of American writing. We are a society strangling in unnecessary words, circular constructions, pompous frills and meaningless jargon.'**
WILLIAM ZINSSER, author

BIN THE ACRONYMS

All companies have their own jargon and acronyms to describe various corporate activities. I was about half an hour into my first day with one employer when a work colleague told me to staple the RD17 to the B303 and then forward them both to PDU. Before long, of course, you learn the lingo and eventually you can even say sentences like that without laughing. The danger is that after a while this language becomes second nature to the extent that we pepper our CV with acronyms that would baffle the average reader and even require a recruitment consultant with a PhD in cryptography to pause for thought.

For further ways to make your CV clear and easy to read, see **IDEA 8, *Cut to the chase*.**

Try another idea...

WHAT'S THAT IN ENGLISH?

I've noticed there's a particular tendency for there to be a rush of linguistic blood to the head when companies come up with names for major change projects. In my time as a management consultant, I've come across change projects called Achieve, Xerxes, Lean Machine and Blue Sky. You rather wish that organisations would either go for something a little more descriptive of the project's purpose (I've always thought that Slash 'n' Burn would work for most organisations) or for a less macho name (wouldn't you love to be put in charge of a change programme called 'Could Be Worse' or 'Mustn't Grumble'?).

'Seven out of ten staff believe that the people they meet outside work judge them instantly by their job titles.'
JOHN VILLIS, recruitment manager

Defining idea...

'I improve on misquotation.'
CARY GRANT

Defining idea...

Feel free not to use the project names that the company comes up with. It will probably make more sense to the reader of your CV if you describe their purpose, perhaps calling them something like 'an organisation-wide change programme focused on cost reduction without job loss' or 'a major change programme designed to improve the company's customer management systems'.

How did it go?

Q **I've tried to remove the jargon from my CV but I found that in some areas jargon is actually the only way to communicate in any depth what I get up to. Is this a problem?**

A *Not necessarily. You don't have to convert everything into Janet and John language that any idiot could understand. There's a distinction between professional jargon and corporate jargon. Corporate jargon is the stuff that only makes sense to other people working in your company. Professional jargon is the language used within, well, professions. It's acceptable to use professional jargon sparingly. The corporate jargon, however, will cause problems.*

Q **I have one of those job titles that means absolutely nothing to most people. I'm therefore more than happy to convert it into something a bit more meaningful, but I'm slightly concerned about the fact that my newly invented job title will appear on reference requests. What should I do about this?**

A *This shouldn't be a problem. When you know that references are about to be taken up, let your new employer have your official job title. Alternatively, drop a short courtesy note to the people you've named as referees letting them know the situation.*

39

Detox your CV

Draw out any harmful content that might raise negative thoughts in the mind of the recruiter.

You don't get two chances to make a first impression. Usually a potential employer will only have your CV (plus maybe a covering letter) on which to base their impression of you.

It's therefore only natural for you to want your CV to look as good as it possibly can. And part of that is about only including information that will make a positive impact on the employer. The reverse side of that particular coin is to excise any information that is likely to impact on the employer negatively.

Here are a few things that your CV will be better off without:

STRIP OUT SURPLUS CONTENT

We've already established that CVs are one-to-one marketing documents. They're about accentuating the positive. Applying for a job isn't the time to strip yourself naked before the CV jury and reveal yourself warts and all. Employers might appreciate your searing honesty, but you'll be unlikely to land an interview.

Here's an idea for you... **Use spellcheck, but remember it won't catch every error. An unnerving example is that if you left the 'l' out of 'public relations', spellcheck will happily nod that through, but the PR Director with the vacancy might be less forgiving!**

Sometimes knowing what to cut out of your CV is a matter of common sense, but sometimes it's a bit more of a judgement call.

In the common-sense category comes all the gratuitous information, i.e. information you've not been asked explicitly to provide that is likely to do your cause more harm than good if you include it. For example, an obsession with extreme sports might keep your stocks of adrenalin high, but it'll probably cause employers a frisson of concern. Likewise, mentioning the penalty points you have on your driving licence can only have a negative impact. Or listing your personal website if it happens to contain pictures of you mooning in Falaraki.

In the judgement call terrain, matters aren't quite so clear-cut. It's more about tone and nuance. Here's an example. Let's say that you're applying for a role that's 100% about dealing with customers face to face. Describing the face-to-face element of your current role ought therefore to get the recruiter's interest. If you devote, say, two bullet points out of four to this facet of your job, it will come over as a substantive part of what you do. However, if those two bullets are out of eight bullets, then you're beginning to dilute their impact by implying that you spend a lot of your time in non-customer-facing activity. Should you place the two bullets in the middle or towards the bottom of the eight, then that will diminish their effect further.

CLEAN UP SPELLING ERRORS

Employers have a nasty habit of assuming that anybody who makes a spelling mistake in their CV is likely to make mistakes on the job. At the very least, you're guilty of a lack of attention to detail.

The following bloopers were all taken from real CVs and covering letters:

- I am very detail-oreinted.
- Graduated in the top 66% of my class.
- Special skills: Thyping.
- Objection: To utilise my skills in sales.
- I am a rabid typist.
- Skills: Operated Pitney Bones machine.
- Strengths: Ability to meet deadlines while maintaining composer.
- Work Experience: Dealing with customers' conflicts that arouse.
- Typing Speed: 756 wpm.

DETOX YOUR QUIRKY INDIVIDUALITY

No photo, no wacky fonts, no coloured paper, no jokes, no eccentric hobbies, no exclamation marks, no personal pronouns, no 'Curriculum Vitae' at the top of each page, no volunteered salary details, no mention of political affiliation, no early schooling details and no unnecessary repetition of facts.

Having de-accentuated the negative, maybe it's time to build up the positive aspects of your CV. Have a look at IDEA 25, *Show some oomph.*

Try another idea...

'The key to any game is to use your strengths and hide your weaknesses.'
PAUL WESTPHAL, former basketball player

Defining idea...

How did
it go?

Q   I think I've stripped out all of the damaging content, but how can I be sure?

A   *In a world that's constantly changing it's hard to be certain that you've excised every last hint of damaging content, but a good starting point is to get someone else to read your CV specifically with an eye out for errors. However, be aware that they too might not spot errors like 'manger' in place of 'manager' because we're inclined to read what we think should be there rather than what actually is there.*

Q   I'm happy that I've fixed any typing errors, but what about detoxing the rest of the content?

A   *Have another read of your CV. Go through it line by line and ask yourself whether each bit of information is relevant to the role you've applied for, deleting anything that fails the test. Then ask yourself whether the information is presented in the right order, with the appropriate weight given to each point. Remember that the more important the information, the nearer to the top of the CV it should be. Any highly relevant information on page two of your CV probably deserves a promotion.*

40

Is your CV fitter than you?

A reminder that although a high impact CV might earn you an interview, it won't get you the job.

Even in these politically correct times, there's ample evidence to suggest that career success is more likely to go to those who look and dress the part.

Had Clint Eastwood's Dirty Harry been a tough-talking HR manager, he would have told us straight: a CV's got to know its limitations. And the big limitation is this. Your CV might be the product of hours of concentrated effort and may have attained a level of visual perfection to match Michelangelo's *David* or Keira Knightley's 'Guinevere'. However, just as the Wizard of Oz, Harry Lime and Harry Potter's adversary Lord Voldemort eventually put in an appearance, so the day will come when you'll need to leave the house and go and talk face to face with a total stranger or two about your suitability to join their organisation.

That's when the rubber really hits the road. All the fine word-smithing in your CV may count for little if you greet your interviewer looking like you have a life-long sponsorship deal with the Lard Marketing Board.

Aim to greet your interviewer confidently, making good eye contact. Try to convey energy and positive enthusiasm. And smile. If you're nervous at the prospect, why not role-play the meeting with a friend?

You never get a second chance to make a first impression. OK, I know it's a cliché, but clichés are often clichés because they're true. Make sure your dress and personal grooming are up to scratch. Seek a (brutally honest) opinion from a friend.

LOOKS COUNT

This might be uncomfortable stuff to take on board, but here are three fairly recent pieces of research that point in various ways to the importance of physical appearance:

1. Physical appearance counts in the workplace, according to a US survey carried out in 2001. People rated as attractive are two to five times more likely to be taken on. They are also less likely to be laid off.

2. A study of 350 firms in Italy found that employees, female and male alike, tend to work better and are more prepared to put in longer hours if they're working for a good-looking, well-groomed boss.

Defining idea...

'Never eat more than you can lift.'
MISS PIGGY

3. Two research studies have found that bald men have less chance of successfully changing jobs than their hirsute colleagues. Researchers created six fictitious CVs, three featuring photographs of men with hair. The other three featured the same three men and the same biographical information, but with their image digitally altered to make them bald. The CVs were then sent to ninety-eight personnel managers along with a batch of genuine applications. Only 27% of the 'bald' candidates were invited to interview compared with 41% of those with hair.

See IDEA 18, *Looks can kill*, for some tips on making your CV easy on the eye.

Try another idea...

Let's keep this in perspective. Workplaces are not packed to the rafters with George Clooney or Cameron Diaz lookalikes. Nor are job centres and outplacement firms overrun with bald, ugly guys. But whether we're female, male or both, it's important that we feel confident about the way we look and the way we dress. When we go to an interview, we need to think about the impression we make.

As a general guideline, it's a better strategy to overdress than underdress. You can always talk your clothes down if you have to; it's far more difficult to talk them clothes up. When you turn up for an interview in a business outfit to be greeted by your new potential boss in a casual sweater, it's plausible to say that you're in your smart clobber because you're off to a formal meeting after the interview. But telling somebody in a smart suit that you're wearing jeans because you're planning to scrub the kitchen floor later that day lacks credibility.

'*Men in general judge more from appearances than from reality. All men have eyes, but few have the gift of penetration.*'
NICOLO MACHIAVELLI

Defining idea...

191

How did it go?

Q   I'll be honest. I'm a man who likes his pies. Is my girth going to come between me and the job of my dreams?

A   *If your girth's proportions will fail a medical then I'm afraid it will. As we become a nation of Teletubbies, a worrying statistic is emerging, namely that growing numbers of people are having their job offers withdrawn because they fail the employer's medical examination. Employers figure that their pension plans are in a bad enough way already without allowing in new employees with a high risk of future health problems. Nor do they want their premises overrun with people who can't communicate without wheezing at the end of every sentence.*

If, on the other hand, you can carry off your extra pounds with aplomb and you cut a decent dash when you're dressed up, you should be OK. It's often down to the state of your self-confidence.

Q   I'm no oil painting. My hair's a mess and my friends tell me I have a terrible dress sense. Should I even bother for a new job?

A   *Now's the time to stay positive. There's always a way to improve your appearance. In the short term, concentrate on what you wear, your hair and make up, personal hygiene, posture, etc. Attention to these areas can yield instant dramatic improvements. In the longer term, healthier eating and taking more exercise might be good strategies.*

41

I'll show you mine if you show me yours

Key to improving our work performance is getting feedback from others on how we're doing. The same principle applies with CVs.

Even if we're our own harshest critic, and let's face it most of us are, there's always merit in paying heed to what we can learn from other people. You'll find feedback everywhere if you listen hard enough.

If we're not careful, crafting a CV can be a solitary pursuit. But once you've put a draft together, resist the temptation to keep it to yourself. Instead, try to get second opinions from people you know. The more feedback you receive before your CV hits the streets, the more likely it is that you'll push the right buttons with your next potential employer.

So, who should you approach? I'd suggest that you choose people from one or more of the following clusters. And if you know individuals who fit into more than one category, so much the better.

Seek the advice of fellow professionals who will be helpful in spotting whether your CV contains all the core elements relating to your line of work, particularly whether you're on top of the latest techniques and buzzwords.

Work colleagues

There's particular value in getting comments from people who know you and the work you're doing. They'll quickly spot any obvious omissions. Also, consider tracking down former work colleagues as they may well recall valuable experience of yours that you've forgotten about.

HR types, recruitment consultants and career consultants

These individuals see more CVs than most so you'd expect them to have gained a few insights. They should also be good at spotting any acronyms and jargon that might be too specialist or company specific.

Networking contacts

The best way to approach networking is to ask the people you contact whether you can tap into their wisdom, expertise and advice. Looking them in the eye and asking them outright for a job will create more resentment than job offers. Seeking feedback on your CV, on the other hand, can be a brilliant basis on which to set up sessions with people on your contacts list. Any feedback from them will obviously be very helpful and if they then spontaneously go on to say that they hadn't appreciated how good you are and would like to offer you a place on the board, so much the better.

Defining idea...

'The secret of creativity is knowing how to hide your sources.'
ALBERT EINSTEIN

LET'S SEE YOURS THEN

Getting feedback on your CV from a range of sources can be incredibly informative and can instigate some useful honing and refining of your proposition. I'm also a patron of the art of creative swiping because it's often possible to draw inspiration from other people's CVs. We might pick up a useful tip or two on any of the following and more: the overall look and layout; the choice and sequencing of sections; a natty turn of phrase that expresses an idea more elegantly than we have; and the font type and size used.

So how can we get to see more of other people's CVs? Well, you're laughing if you work in HR, but some of the following might work for the rest of us:

■ Keep an eye out for any speculative CVs that turn up in your work area.
■ Volunteer to help out with a recruitment exercise.
■ If you're one of a bunch of people who's been made redundant, try forming a job club and sharing ideas and experience.
■ Simply ask people if they have a CV and whether you can have a look at it!

The point is, it's not cheating to draw on other people's best practice. Remember that your CV scores points for conveying your story effectively and you're unlikely to be asked at interview whether you wrote your CV unaided.

Try another idea...

IDEA 43, *Networking*, will help you put together and build on a very useful collection of contacts.

Defining idea...

'A woman tells her doctor, "I've got a bad back." The doctor says, "It's old age." The woman says, "I want a second opinion." The doctor says, "OK, you're ugly as well."'
TOMMY COOPER, fez-sporting comic genius

How did
it go?

Q **Some of the feedback I've received regarding my CV has been useful, but some I just don't agree with. What should I do now?**

A *That's the trouble with feedback. Sometimes it confirms our world view and sometimes it just doesn't compute with us. I think it was Lady Thatcher who once drew a distinction between ministers and advisers by saying that the role of advisers was to advise whereas the role of ministers was to decide. The same thing applies here really. You're the ultimate arbiter of what does and doesn't go into your CV, although I'd caution against discounting every opinion that doesn't fit neatly with your own way of thinking. I'd be particularly inclined to listen if a particular piece of feedback is echoed by a number of people. They might be wrong, but they're more likely to have a point.*

Q **I showed my CV to a friend yesterday and got some useful tips. She's now asked me for some feedback on her CV. There's a few things I don't like about it, but I don't want to offend her. What do you advise?**

A *There are plenty of books about giving feedback and it might be an idea to have a look at one before you wade in. Some general principles are that feedback should be positive, constructive, specific, factual and based on best practice rather than personal opinion.*

42
Quality versus quantity

Which of the following approaches do you think works better? Sending your CV out on a carefully targeted basis or spamming it to all and sundry?

Chumming: The indiscriminate distribution of one's CV in the hope of attracting the interest of somebody important.

If your letterbox is anything like mine, it's admitting more and more junk mail. The amount of material I receive that I can consign unopened to the recycling pile beggars belief. Yet I can understand why finance companies and the rest of them do it – for every ninety-eight of us that they annoy (to varying degrees), two people might show a slither of interest. That's the business model. The cost of the ninety-eight is lower than the profit that stems from the two.

Strategy one: Flood the market
It is possible to take this business model and apply it to the job market. Pick up a copy of the *Yellow Pages*, start at the letter 'A', send off a hundred speculative letters accompanied by your CV and you might get a couple of nibbles. Tomorrow, move onto 'B', and so on.

Here's an idea for you... **If you already have a sturdy network in place, aim to double the number of contacts you have over the next six months.**

Such a strategy may not be a bad idea at a time when new figures from the Chartered Institute of Personnel and Development's annual recruitment and retention survey reveal that 85% of employers have experienced difficulties in recruiting in the last year. Against that backdrop, it's just that little bit more likely that your unsolicited approach might be a solution to a company's recruitment problem.

The downside is that it's quite a labour-intensive approach. One hundred copies of your CV, accompanied by a hundred covering letters – each of which needs to identify a named recipient in the company – is quite a production run, particularly if you're using the home inkjet. On top of that there's addressing the envelopes, sorting the cost of postage and taking the whole caboodle to a postbox.

Strategy two: Don't flood the market

This strategy is based on the premise that we shouldn't be fooled into thinking that posting off one hundred job applications is necessarily any better than sending ten.

When we look at the stats for how vacancies are actually filled, research by some of the big outplacement companies suggests that as many as two-thirds are filled on the back of networking. Recruitment agencies and press advertisements account for another 30% or so. Speculative approaches bring in only around one to two per cent of new recruits.

These figures suggest that we're better off spending our time on working and building our contacts, talking to agencies and responding to specific advertisements rather than engaging in mass mail-outs. With this approach, we concentrate on fewer opportunities but we pursue them more thoroughly than is possible with an out-and-out speculative strategy. By thoroughly, I mean that we produce a tailored covering letter and that we intentionally rejig our CV to match what we have to offer as closely as possible to what we believe the organisation wants.

I suggest that you consult IDEA 9, *Throw another log on the file*, for some tips on putting together a monitoring system for all the applications you have on the go.

Try another idea...

Strategy three: The best of both worlds

On the one hand, putting our energy into a small number of targeted approaches seems to deliver better results. On the other hand, when you're seriously looking to change jobs, it's good for the morale to have a number of applications on the go at any given time. So perhaps the ideal approach is to strike a balance between quality and quantity. In other words, to go for a targeted approach that attempts to have a number of strong options on the go, but not so many as to make them indiscriminate. To put it another way, successful job-hunting isn't a matter of quality or quantity, but quality *and* quantity.

Nobody said this was going to be a doddle!

'It is the quality of our work which will please God and not the quantity.'
MAHATMA GANDHI

Defining idea...

Q **I've been looking at journals and websites, and jobs in my field seem very thin on the ground. What can I do to pep up my job search?**

A *Don't forget the national press, recruitment agencies and above all networking. Tapping into and extending your network could well yield results, bearing in mind that two out of three roles are reputedly filled by that route. Building a good relationship with the recruitment agencies can also work well. The real secret of successful job-hunting is to pursue as many avenues as you can manage.*

Q **I've found my dream job and I'm now finding it hard to summon the energy to pursue less attractive options. Is this the norm?**

A *Don't single-mindedly pursue one vacancy to the exclusion of everything else. Always aim to have a number of possibilities on the go. It'll be fantastic if you get this job, but bear in mind that if you don't then you'll be back to square one, with not only the disappointment of missing out to contend with, but also no other irons in the fire to redirect your energy towards.*

43

Networking

There's more to networking than fishing out all the business cards you've accumulated over the years. Besides, exemplary networking is about quality of contacts not quantity.

Getting your network operating effectively is undoubtedly an essential component of the job-hunting process. In fact, outplacement consultants believe that as many as two-thirds of all job moves come about on the back of networking.

In one episode of *The Simpsons* Homer tries to get his boss (Mr Burns) to remember his name. Finally he resorts to writing 'I am Homer Simpson' on the wall of Mr Burns's office, at which point Mr Burns walks in, switches on the lights and says, 'Who the devil are you?' Perhaps not the most constructive way to register your existence with other people.

Networking has been defined as 'all the different ways in which people make, and are helped to make, connections with each other'. It sometimes gets a bad press from those who see it as a variation on the old boy network. However, as traditional formal hierarchies have died away and we become increasingly mobile in our careers, networking is more important than ever.

Here's an idea for you...

Concentrate on getting in touch with a handful of extremely well-connected people. Don't simply go through your contacts resolutely from A to Z. Ask yourself who your 'platinum' contacts are and establish when you're going to get in touch with them.

There are four main types of network:

- Personal (e.g. friends, relations, neighbours)
- Work (e.g. present and past bosses, colleagues, customers and suppliers)
- Professional (e.g. solicitors, accountants, bank managers, shop owners, doctors)
- Organisations (e.g. professional associations and clubs, chambers of commerce)

And here are six tips on how to build and maintain a set of contacts that will open doors:

Defining idea...

'There are four ways, and only four ways, in which we have contact with the world. We are evaluated and classified by these four contacts: what we do, how we look, what we say, and how we say it.'
DALE CARNEGIE

1. Take the time and effort to build and nurture a network.
There's a book on networking by Harvey Mackay called *Dig Your Well Before You're Thirsty*, which makes the point that you can't make use of a network until you've put one in place, so it makes sense to be constantly developing your contacts.

2. Manage your network on an ongoing basis.
Having somebody's business card tucked away in your desk drawer doesn't necessarily mean that that person is a fully signed up member of your network. Here's the acid test: could you pick up the phone and call them right now without them struggling to remember you or taking umbrage? Let's put it another way: if you got a call from a fellow delegate on a course you went on ten years ago and you

could barely remember them, how much help would you realistically want to be to them? As a broad rule of thumb, if you haven't had any contact with somebody for at least six months, it may be presumptuous to assume they're part of your network.

A prerequisite of good networking is to know exactly what you're after. IDEA 5, *Me in a nutshell*, should help to remind you of what you're trying to achieve.

Try another idea...

3. Be clear about what you're trying to achieve.

The more focused the message you feed into a network, the better the chance that something might come of it. 'I'm looking for a senior project management role in the pharmaceutical industry' is far more likely to register memorably and positively with people than 'I'm ready to move on. Not sure what I'm looking for to be honest. Fancy a bit of a change if truth be told, but beggars can't be choosers.'

4. Get your network on your side.

Don't antagonise your contacts by seeming to exploit your relationship with them. It's far more effective to ask people if you can tap into their advice and guidance than to look them in the eye and ask them outright for a job.

5. Make use of your network's network.

You can widen your network by using existing contacts to give you the names of other useful people.

6. Keep a record of who you contact and when.

When somebody gives you their business card, jot down on the back of the card where and when you met them.

'Eth: If Ron doesn't mix with better-class people, how's he going to get on in life? In this world, it's not what you know, it's who you know, isn't it Ron? Ron: Yes Eth, and I don't know either of them.'
FRANK MUIR and DENIS NORDEN, from BBC Radio's *The Glums*

Defining idea...

How did
it go?

Q   **I'd like to network more, but I only have a handful of useful contacts. How should I go about it?**

A   *The secret is not to take your network at face value. Could you diversify your contacts? For example, if you know just five people in each of those four main categories I mentioned (personal, work, professionals and organisations) and those five people can each connect you to five more people, that's one hundred people already.*

Q   **That all sounds very energy sapping. Isn't there an easier or less intensive way to network?**

A   *You have a point – to a degree. There are avid networkers I know who have three thousand people on their Christmas card list; for 95% of those people, that card is the only point of contact every year. I get cards every year from mystery well-wishers that I probably met at a function months or years ago. I can't imagine that it's at all productive for them. I know that it's damned annoying for me. If you don't have a passion for networking, leave the bulk buying of Christmas cards to others and concentrate on a few high-value contacts instead. They could be the president or chair of a particular society or group, or even somebody who has particular good contacts in a company you'd love to work for.*

44

Perfect your personal elevator pitch

How to use your CV as a basis for developing a succinct and memorable personal 'commercial' that will register you positively with other people.

Let's face it, the question on everyone's lips on meeting somebody for the first time is more often than not, 'So what do you do then?'

There we are, say, at a party or a wedding and one of the first ways we try to pin down the person we're talking with is to find out what they do for a living. In these more egalitarian times, we're not necessarily that bothered about whether we're talking with a captain of industry or a plumber – we just want to know. Perhaps, like me, however, you've occasionally been at the receiving end of a brain-numbingly dull answer to that question, where the only point of interest is how long you can last before that oops-there-goes-my-will-to-live moment.

Here are a few pointers for when you first meet someone:

1. Smile. Not too fleetingly (can seem insincere) or for too long (can look a tad manic).

Here's an idea for you... **Don't try to define yourself too literally. International speaker and networking guru Roy Sheppard believes that we need to go well beyond our job titles and identify what results we create. Consider the difference between saying 'I'm a professional one-to-one career coach' and 'I help people build better careves and lives for themselves'.**

2. Offer your right hand positively to invite a handshake. This is generally a good idea, but don't bother if the other party has a plate in one hand and a drink in the other.

3. Always expect to offer your name first when kicking off a conversation. People like to know who they're talking with and will generally tell you who they are in return. If you come across somebody and you think you've met before, still offer your name first to put them at ease (they might be struggling to remember your name).

4. If somebody else introduces you to an acquaintance of theirs, make sure you're happy with the way they did it. For example, following an introduction along the lines of 'And this old reprobate is my chum and drinking buddy John, who claims to be a bit of a writer', you might want to chip in with something a bit more formal.

You now have the chance to offer up some conversational bait to make a positive impression on the other person. You can make something up on the spot if you wish, but if you really want to impress, don't rely on your ability to spontaneously come up with a compelling self-description.

Instead, I'd recommend that you try to come up with a short (30 seconds or less), sharp and interesting way of describing yourself. Take the time to write down your answer and then take the time to read it. Your aim is to light up the eyes of a prospective client or command a vote of confidence from a satisfied past client. If your self-introduction makes you yawn, then you can expect to bore the pants off all the people you meet too. So, it's worth giving this some serious thought and making a serious effort to imagine and develop yourself as a brand.

You might want to start by identifying the qualities or characteristics that make you distinctive from your competitors and even your colleagues. What would people (colleagues, customers, etc.) say is your greatest strength or your most noteworthy personal trait? To put the challenge succinctly, ask yourself what you want to be known for. Work out the answer to that and you'll be well on the way to creating your elevator pitch.

Meeting people is one thing. Remembering when and where is another. IDEA 9, *Throw another log on the file*, provides advice on keeping a networking log.

Try another idea...

'*If you think of your CV as an elevator pitch – the kind of punchy and concise delivery you have to give when you're selling something – you begin to realise that the formal list of jobs and qualifications to which we have become accustomed needs to be reordered.*'
BILL FAUST, co-author of *Pitch Yourself*, from an interview he gave about his book in the *Financial Times*

Defining idea...

How did it go?

Q   I tried my elevator pitch the other day and it was a disaster. I'm not at all comfortable with the idea. Besides, I work at home and live in a bungalow! Is it really worth it?

A   *I'm detecting a wee bit of resistance here! The idea of proclaiming what makes us so good to a partial or complete stranger doesn't always come naturally. Nevertheless, like any new habit, it will become more comfortable the more you do it. Funnily enough, we often have more trouble giving our pitch to an individual than to a group of individuals. I suspect that when we introduce ourselves to a group, there's more of a performance element involved which in turn makes us feel a little less personally exposed.*

Q   I'm now quite comfortable with giving my pitch to groups, but I still stumble a bit when I'm talking one to one. Do you have any more suggestions?

A   *The first option is to practise, practise, practise, practise. Practise in front of a mirror. Practise into a voice recorder. Just try to make it a perfectly work-a-day thing in your life. Eventually you'll shift from being consciously incompetent to being unconsciously competent! The second option is to slightly change the way you launch your elevator pitch. The next time somebody wants to know who you are and what you do, simply kick off with, 'What I normally tell people who ask that question is that...' and then slip into your pitch. Sounds bizarre I know, but it means that instead of delivering your pitch directly to somebody, you're putting your response in quotation marks. Many people I know feel more comfortable with this.*

45

Dealing with specialist recruiters

The way to get the best results out of your dealings with specialist recruiters is to build and manage a relationship with them. So here's how to go about wooing them.

Professional recruiters fall into four categories: high street agencies, headhunters, search and selection businesses, and interim agencies.

High street agencies normally deal in the more junior posts and temporary positions. Aside from directly applying to companies, they are the most worthwhile point of contact for anybody seeking manual, administrative or secretarial roles.

Headhunters are commissioned by companies to find senior executives with a particular set of attributes. They assemble a shortlist of people with the best fit and receive a fee (usually equivalent to a sizeable percentage of the first year's salary). The shortlist is often a combination of candidates who respond to advertisements placed by the headhunters, people who have directly approached the headhunters and those sought out by the headhunting company because of a recommendation from another party.

Here's an idea for you... **Get your interview technique match fit before you meet up with any specialist recruiters. Practise, rehearse, become comfortable with telling your career story, including why you're putting yourself on the job market at this point. Think of the questions you'd least like to be asked and come up with some convincing responses.**

Search and selection businesses focus on middle to senior level jobs. Their clients are a combination of people responding to advertisements and those who approach them directly.

Interim management agencies focus on providing senior executives to companies who need them to take on a significant assignment for a limited period, on average around six months. As with search and selection businesses, their clients come from two sources: people responding to advertisements and direct approaches.

GETTING YOUR CV IN THEIR HANDS

Whereas high street agencies are happy for people to walk in off the street, most headhunters, interim agencies and search and selection businesses prefer to receive a CV first, which will be followed by a meeting if appropriate. That said, walking in off the street to personally deliver a CV and then asking for a few minutes of somebody's time can be a highly productive way of registering your presence in the market.

BUILDING A RELATIONSHIP

Professional recruiters are client-driven, not candidate-driven, i.e. they consider themselves to be working primarily for companies and not for you. As a result, it can often feel like you're getting a poor service from them. You may find they often claim to be too busy to talk to you, which can be a little galling given that they stand to make a sizeable commission out of placing you with a company.

The key to a successful relationship is for you to take responsibility for both the service they provide and for managing how the relationship develops. So, don't risk dropping off their radar by assuming they're being active on your behalf and putting you forward for lots of jobs. It's worth calling them every ten days or so to see what's around. Even though you're registered with them, when you see an advertisement they have placed that interests you, contact them to explicitly state your interest in being considered for the post.

Specialist recruiters are geared up to keep you doing what you've always been doing. Is that what you want? Remind yourself with another peek at IDEA 1, *Dream a little dream.*

 Try another idea...

'You put your paycheck, your money, in the bank so it can be managed by someone else...Whatever you do with it, you place it in someone else's hands so you can focus on what you do best. There is nothing different about using a good head-hunter to help you invest your employable assets.'
DARRELL W. GURNEY, author of *Head-hunters Revealed!*

Defining idea...

'I think that we may safely trust a good deal more than we do. We may waive just so much care of ourselves as we honestly bestow elsewhere.'
HENRY DAVID THOREAU

You can use your CV as a tool for maintaining a relationship as well. As we've discussed elsewhere, a CV is a permanent work in progress. As you produce new variations or substantial revisions of your CV, use that new CV as a reason to phone or call in to see them.

GIVING THEM WHAT THEY WANT

In order to sell you to companies, agencies need to know what makes you a bit better than the rest of the competition. For that reason, they're particularly keen to see your career achievements, supported by a clear outline of companies worked for, jobs held, key responsibilities and the relevant dates. They'll normally edit your CV to match their house style for presenting information about clients to companies. For that reason, you don't need to stick slavishly to the two-page format.

By the way, agencies tend not to be big fans of the functional CV. This is because they'll be more at home selling you into a very similar role to the one you're moving away from. They'll be much less comfortable with helping you to achieve a significant change in career direction.

Q **I've been asked if I'm interested in interim work, but I don't feel I understand it well enough to answer this. Can you fill me in?**

How did it go?

A *Let's build on what you already know. It's estimated that there are around 30,000 interim managers operating in the UK, so this is definitely a worthwhile alternative to looking for a permanent job. As well as being used in an emergency, interim managers are increasingly being used for planned assignments. When it comes to change management, they're often favoured over consultants and permanent staff. It's said that they differ from consultants because typically the interim manager is there to implement rather than recommend.*

Q **How should I play a meeting with an interim management agency?**

A *A key thing to remember when talking with interim agencies is to stress your absolute commitment to the interim lifestyle. If you say that you're also exploring permanent options, they'll assume that you regard interim work as a second choice, which simply won't cut it with the agency. In terms of what they'll be looking for in you, expect to be quizzed closely about your achievements and about your ability to hit the ground running. Interim assignments are short, sharp, intensive bursts of activity with no real time for a learning curve.*

215

46

Handling interviews

A CV has only really achieved its goal if you secure an interview, when you'll need to reinforce and build on its content.

If your CV isn't securing you interviews, then you might as well wrap your old potato peelings in it and lob it in a bin for all the use it is to you and your career.

If you're invited to an interview, you'll normally have a week or two's notice. This period is a crucial part of the proceedings. Used effectively, you can give yourself a real chance to shine on the day.

At this point I'd like to remind you of something glaringly obvious, but hugely important. The reason you've been offered an interview is because somebody liked what you put into your CV. The content will have struck them as relevant, interesting and at the very least sufficiently intriguing to suggest you might have something useful to offer.

So, when you go along to an interview, be ready to expand on each and every element of your CV. Every line, every point you make, every comma is a legitimate

Identify the key points you want to get across at an interview and take a mental checklist along with you to the meeting.

subject of conversation with your interviewer (OK, maybe not the commas unless you've applied to the Society for the Prevention of Cruelty to Commas or similar).

REFRESH YOUR KNOWLEDGE OF YOUR CV

All the achievement statements, for example, that make an appearance in your CV are entirely legitimate topics for the interviewer to explore, which means that if you want to impress the interviewer, you'll need to be able to expand on this information. So, refresh your memory about each achievement so that you have all the relevant details at your fingertips.

I've conducted interviews where the candidate has been asked about a particular project referred to in the CV. Hardly a trick question and yet people stumble over basic facts and figures. I remember one exchange that went something like this:

'It's the first time I've opened a pier. Nothing can really prepare you, though last night I opened a tin of tomatoes and then declared my bathroom open.'
STEPHEN FRY, comedian, giving his backing to the principle of being prepared when he opened Cromer Pier in the summer of 2004

Candidate: The project started in April 1998…actually, it was July. Anyway, the project had three key aims…(candidate only remembers two of them)…and it completed in May 1999.
Interviewer: Oh, you say in your CV that it finished in August 1999.
Candidate: Swipe me, you're right!

Now the odd slip of the tongue or the memory is understandable at an interview, as nerves often play a part. But let's face it, you were the one who mentioned the project in the first place, so it's hardly the interviewer's fault if they want to know a little bit more about it.

DON'T CREATE HOSTAGES TO FORTUNE

Something you absolutely want to avoid is putting anything in your CV where you've slightly buffed up the truth to make your contribution seem more impressive than it really was. When you're sat at your computer compiling your CV and there's a job requirement mentioned in the advertisement that you don't meet as strongly as you'd like, it's quite tempting to deploy just a smidgen of exaggeration. After all, where's the real harm in that?

Well, the harm becomes very evident when you find yourself blathering and blustering at an interview because you can't back up the substance of your CV. And the trouble is that an interviewer who uncovers just one chink in your credibility will not be inclined to believe that the rest of your CV is a chink-free zone.

So far, I've concentrated on how your CV can influence your interview performance, because CVs are the focus of this book. However, you might well want to seek out some more comprehensive advice on preparation and performance to supplement this perspective. In the meantime, here are a few general tips for optimising your interview performance:

- Anticipate what the interviewer(s) might want to know about you.
- Prepare a few questions to ask at the end of the interview.
- Appear positive and enthusiastic. At the end of the interview, explicitly confirm your interest in the job.

Try another idea…

Don't scupper your chances of interview success by sexing up your CV and being exposed as somebody who dresses up the truth. Read more about this in **IDEA 13, *Ditch the dodgy dossier.***

Defining idea…

'*I refuse to answer that question on the grounds that I don't know the answer.*'
DOUGLAS ADAMS

219

How did it go?

Q **I've tried to find out what I can about the company I have an interview with tomorrow, but there's not much to go on. Is there anything I can do at the last minute?**

A Take a cultural sounding by arriving early, sitting in reception and observing what goes on. Were you expected? Did you get a friendly greeting and the offer of a cup of coffee? What sort of conversations did they have with colleagues passing by? Also, watch out for any company literature. A front page of the company newsletter devoted to a team of the month award, for example, will tell you something about the organisation's values and aspirations. On the other hand, if the front page is devoted to a dry-as-tinder address by the CEO exhorting the troops to tighten their belts, it's another clear, if less positive, indication of what you might be letting yourself in for.

Q **What's the advice these days for handling the interview question that asks about weaknesses?**

A When asked to describe a weakness, it's not clever to come back with 'I can't think of one.' You'll be marked down as lacking self-knowledge at best and as an arrogant so-and-so at worst. Once upon a time, the best answer was to offer a weakness that was a strength in disguise. For example, 'I'm not too good at time management as I'll always take time out to help a colleague who's struggling. As a result, I sometimes fall a bit behind with my own workload, although I'll always stay late that day if I need to catch up.' Responses like this – sometimes called 'the noble weakness' – can still work well. These days, however, it's reckoned that refreshing honesty like 'My spelling's abysmal' might just be the best policy, unless your weakness is so grave as to scare the interviewer off.

47

Handling rejection

A rejection letter needn't be the end of the story. A good follow-up strategy can keep you in the corporate mind's eye.

As one of my friends puts it, rejection is life's way of saying 'Not yet'. Admittedly, my friend has a very optimistic disposition, but there are real benefits in not taking rejection too hard.

Picture this scenario. You've had the interview. It seemed to go well and you came away thinking that you could enjoy working there. You go home and await the outcome of the interview only to be told that – stab my vitals – the organisation has opted to go for another candidate. At this point, you can adopt for one of three dispositions:

1. Stoically take it on the chin and focus on the next application.

2. Unleash a volley of foul-mouthed bile to the effect that the interviewer and in fact the entire company should be dropped down a sizeable hole and forgotten about until the end of time.

Keep a record of every vacancy you apply for. When an application comes to the end of the road (for example, if you're not shortlisted or if you're interviewed but not offered the job), jot down a note of any lessons you've learned from that particular application.

3. Turn rejection into an opportunity to build something for the future.

The first two dispositions are both understandable at a human level, but they treat a rejection as the end of the road. The third disposition suggests that all may not be lost. Someone of the third disposition will recognise that success in the job search process is typically not about being head and shoulders above all other candidates – it's about striving to be a few per cent better than the competition every step of the way.

Examples of how to gain that advantage include: having a CV that conveys your experience and achievements more effectively; researching a company that bit more thoroughly; being that bit better prepared for the interview; making a better first impression at interview than others; and, critically in this context, following up key stages of the selection process more effectively than others. So, for example, when you get back home after an interview consider dropping a line to the interviewer to say that you enjoyed the interview and reconfirm your interest in the job. This is also your opportunity to enclose any information or material that you discussed at the interview and may have promised to provide.

If you're not offered a particular job, think seriously about asking for some feedback on your performance. You could also write to the interviewer(s). Perhaps send something along the lines of: 'Thank you for letting me know the outcome of my recent interview. Obviously I'm disappointed not to have been offered the job, as I would have greatly relished taking on this challenging and exciting role. I'd like to take this chance to reaffirm my genuine interest in your organisation and to ask you to bear me in mind for any suitable vacancies that might arise in the future.'

If you skipped past IDEA 46, *Handling interviews*, turn back to find some suggestions that will reduce your chances of receiving that 'no thanks' letter.

Try another idea...

Gratuitous toadying? I don't think so. You're simply bringing this particular episode to a close whilst leaving channels of communication open. The organisation will think well of you for doing this and who knows what might come of it. Moreover, for a whole host of reasons the vacancy may reoccur. What if the candidate they offered the job to gets an even better offer from somewhere else or finds that the family don't want to relocate? If this happens, then obviously there are no guarantees, but at least you've left yourself well positioned for the organisation to come back to you.

'That which does not kill me makes me stronger.'
FREDERICK NIETZSCHE

Defining idea...

223

How did it go?

Q   **The job I wanted has been offered to another candidate who's accepted the position. Can you put a positive spin on that?**

A   *I certainly can! Look, it's only natural to feel disappointed. These days, the typical selection process can often involve assessment centres and a number of interviews so the emotional investment can be high. But when all is said and done, you have a choice now. You can never speak to the company again or you can try to salvage something positive from the experience. A polite note thanking them for their interest in you and reinforcing your interest in them leaves your relationship with them on a good footing and you never know where that might lead.*

Q   **Can you give an example of where that might lead?**

A   *Imagine another candidate has accepted their offer. They then get a better offer from another organisation or decide not to turn up for duty. Or they decide after a little while that the job isn't for them and leave after six months. Or what if the company has a similar role that becomes available? In any of these cases, the organisation could turn to you without having to go through the whole rigmarole of another advertisement and recruitment process.*

48

Avoiding the poisoned chalice

Tips on how to avoid 'Titanic' projects, plus what to put in your CV if you can't avoid the looming icebergs.

As organisations set up more and more project teams to tackle corporate problem areas, we need to be able to differentiate between the career-enhancing projects and those that should be avoided like the plague.

The same goes for the jobs we hold. Some will set us fair for a place on the board while others might poison our career. The trick is to know which is which.

Remember this famous scene from Danny Kaye's 1956 classic *The Court Jester*?

Hawkins: I've got it! I've got it! The pellet with the poison's in the vessel with the pestle; the chalice from the palace has the brew that is true! Right?
Griselda: Right. But there's been a change: they broke the chalice from the palace!

Here's an idea for you...

Accentuate any positive elements of a project that has failed to deliver the goods. However, if 'bleeding disaster' is the only term that applies, devote very little space to it and emphasise the personal learning that has come out of failure. Also remember that your most recent work will take priority over projects you were involved with in the distant past.

Hawkins: They broke the chalice from the palace?
Griselda: And replaced it with a flagon.
Hawkins: A flagon...?
Griselda: With the figure of a dragon.
Hawkins: Flagon with a dragon.
Griselda: Right.
Hawkins: But did you put the pellet with the poison in the vessel with the pestle?
Griselda: No!!! The pellet with the poison's in the flagon with the dragon! The vessel with the pestle has the brew that is true!
Hawkins: The pellet with the poison's in the flagon with the dragon; the vessel with the pestle has the brew that is true.
Griselda: Just remember that.

Trying to spot the chalice from the palace that will serve our careers well isn't always easy. Here are a few tips regarding what to watch out for:

PERFECT VERSUS POISONOUS PROJECTS

A high proportion of the interesting work going on in organisations today comes in bite-sized chunks called projects. Broadly speaking this is good news for you and your CV. A project-based career enables you to grow your skill set, your record of achievement and your corporate reputation more rapidly than any other method. As management guru Tom Peters once put it: 'Projects exist around deliverables, they create measurables, and they leave you with braggables. If you're not spending at least 70% of your time working on projects, creating projects or organising your (apparently mundane) tasks into projects, you are sadly living in the past. Today you have to think, breathe, act and work in projects.'

Have a look at IDEA 21, *Another skeleton, another cupboard: redundancy*, to see that all is far from lost in disheartening situations.

Try another idea...

There's no doubt that being involved in a project with high stakes and a high status can give you real career momentum. If the project has a high-quality leader, has full backing from the top management team and possibly some world-class consultants supporting the pursuit of project objectives, which are themselves realistic, measurable and potentially high impact, then there's an excellent chance for your CV to be enhanced significantly.

On the other hand, being seconded to a poorly led project with no substantive backing from the top team can leave you floundering in the organisational margins. Actually, things might get even worse. Your old bosses might take the view that the temporary arrangement put in place to cover your job while you're away in project land worked rather more effectively than you ever did and they don't want you back, which could leave you floating in corporate limbo-land until the next wave of job cuts identifies you as being surplus to requirements.

'These three little sentences will get you through life: Number 1: Oh, good idea boss. Number 2: Cover for me. Number 3: It was like that when I got here.'
HOMER SIMPSON providing some fatherly advice to Bart

Defining idea...

Defining idea...

The key to making projects work for you is to put yourself forward every time you sniff out a project with a high chance of meaningful success. Here are some specifics that might work for you:

- Let it be widely known that you have a lot of respect for the Project Director.
- Put together a version of your CV highlighting what you could bring to the project.
- Convince your current manager that your getting involved in the project would be a great opportunity to hand some added responsibility to some of your more promising colleagues.

On the other hand, where you detect the foul whiff of failure around a project, keep your head down!

Q **I've just been invited to join Project Cataclysm. As you might imagine, I'm not keen, so I tried to keep my head down, but that didn't work. Any idea how I can get out of this one?**

How did it go?

A *If a project team is keener on you than you are on them, try playing one or more of the following 'Get Out of Jail Free' cards:*

Look to convince your boss that times are very busy and that now isn't the right time to release you.

Point to your work team's current lack of experience and your concerns for hitting departmental targets.

If there's a mini-project that you've been meaning to put in place back at the ranch, now's the time to get it up and running.

Try to persuade people that you could make a more meaningful contribution to a different project, i.e. one that has a better chance of success.

Q **I've tried all of the above and nothing worked this time round. Do you have anything else up your sleeve?**

A *Try to arrange for your involvement to be on a part-time basis. This allows you to continue to show your day job on your CV as your primary activity and you'll be able to really play down your role in Project Cataclysm. If this fails and you're really convinced the project is going nowhere, then maybe it's time to start job-hunting.*

49

Manage the brand called You

A unique selling point will make you stand out from the crowd. So, what makes you so special?

What particular combination of skills and experience might give you an edge over others going for the same job?

'It's this simple: you are a brand. You are in charge of your brand. There is no single path to success. And there is no one right way to create the brand called You. Except this: Start today. Or else.'

That's a quote from Tom Peters, probably the world's best known (and best paid) management guru, in an article called 'The Brand Called You: You Can't Move Up If You Don't Stand Out' that he wrote for *Fast Company* magazine in August 1997. In a nutshell, the article proposed that we should manage our career as though it were a brand. Peters proposed that like a classic marketing brand, our personal brand value can rise or fall depending on how well we nurture and manage our brand and how well we perform in the marketplace.

Take England footballer Wayne Rooney, for example. Football commentators reckon that his performances during the Euro 2004 tournament increased his value in the transfer market fourfold. Imagine how much more he would have been worth if he hadn't tripped over his own boot and broken a bone in his foot!

Here's an idea for you...

Ask yourself the following deceptively simple question to help you define your brand: What do I want to be famous for? Then ask yourself what needs to happen next in order for you to get closer to your chosen brand identity.

But this isn't just a concept to apply to people with a high media profile. You may cringe at the thought of being 'a brand called You' or 'Chief Executive of Me', but behind this clodhopping language rests a new truth about what lays ahead for everyone looking to change jobs.

To put it bluntly, getting a new job isn't the challenge. Finding the right job is, however. Whether you're contemplating an internal or external move, you need to make sure that it keeps your career moving in an upward trajectory. Choose the right employer and that can increase your brand value. Choose the wrong employer and you can do lasting damage to your earning potential.

So, what can we do to protect our careers?

ACTIVELY MANAGE YOUR CAREER

I can sympathise if reading this stuff is making you feel like a lie-down, but please don't be like most of your colleagues, who probably manage their careers on the hoof. The trouble is, the general assumption seems to be that performing well in a given job is all that matters. In other words, look after your job and somehow your career will take care of itself. Not true. Building a long and successful career requires a 'planned maintenance' mentality. Don't assume that combining patience with a dollop of opportunism will do the trick – bugger all

Defining idea...

'**In a nutshell, the key to success is identifying unique modules of talent within you and then finding the right arena in which to use them.**'
WARREN BENNIS, author and social philosopher

comes to they who wait. Or to quote my favourite Chinese proverb: 'A peasant must stand a long time on a hillside with his mouth wide open before a roast duck flies in.'

KEEP YOUR HANDS ON THE WHEEL

Don't entrust your career to anybody. Don't rely on the company's Management Development Manager or VP-Succession Planning to look after your interests – they have other fish to fry. And don't rely on your current boss to look after your best interests. Now I admit that I may be doing them a grave disservice, but all too many managers are very happy to keep their good people for as long as they possibly can.

Here's the acid test: has your boss ever said anything to you along the lines of 'I'm concerned that you're not spending enough time planning your next job move. You should be keeping an eye out for the right opportunity. Oh, and start networking more'? Paradoxically, if your boss has been saying that to you, it's probably because they think you're rubbish at your job and they're desperate to shuffle you off the premises.

AIM HIGH

Finally, don't imagine that the skills, knowledge and experience that got you where you are today will be sufficient to propel you where you want to be in the future. Seek out opportunities to acquire new skills, become a voracious learner and develop career purpose. People with a vision of their future and goals linked to that vision are far more likely to succeed than those who don't.

Have another look at IDEA 5, *Me in a nutshell*, to help you assess whether your CV trumpets your brand. You might also want to have a look at IDEA 25, *Show some oomph*, if you feel your CV needs an injection of energy.

Try another idea...

'You don't have an old-fashioned résumé anymore! You've got a marketing brochure for brand You.'
TOM PETERS, management guru

Defining idea...

233

How did it go?

Q **I'm struggling to put this idea into practice. Can you provide a few practical pointers on how I can build my brand value?**

A *Personal brand building happens over months and years rather than days and weeks. You'll need to commit quite a bit of time and energy to the process. In a magazine article, Tom Peters gave five tips:*

1. *Find a mentor: Time was when mentors used to pick their protégés, these days, protégés are likely to be picking their mentors.*

2. *Look the part: Dress in a style that suits your job, and which matches people's expectations.*

3. *Become an active member of your professional association: It will increase your professional know-how and help you build an impressive set of contacts.*

4. *Specialise: Be the person that everybody turns to when the budget needs checking, or the computer goes wrong, or when people want a good listener.*

5. *Develop your presentation skills.*

Q **These all seem like useful short-term steps to take, but what about in the longer term?**

A *The most important thing is to have a vision: think hard about your goals and how you're going to achieve them.*

50

Do you even need a CV at all?

The nature of our work dictates whether we need a CV to further our careers. That said, we might need one even if we think we don't. Confused? Then read on.

Some of us know exactly what we're trying to achieve in terms of our careers. For example, our goal might be to have a place on the board by the time we're a certain age.

Alternatively, we might want to be employed by a certain organisation or to work our socks off so that we can retire early from the rat race.

This clarity acts as a touchstone for all our career-related decisions. Unfortunately, not all of us, quite possibly very few of us in reality, have that level of clarity. We work just as hard at every job we hold as those who do have a strong sense of career direction, but we're pursuing no real game plan and our whole career progress is more of a glorious accident.

Here's an idea for you... **Gather together assorted materials that you can use to create a sculpture of your career to date. Make your sculpture and reflect on what it says about your career to date and perhaps your aspirations for the future. Then read your CV and ask yourself how effectively your current CV reflects your sculpture.**

Take me, for instance. I left college in the 1970s and bummed around for a bit before moving from Somerset to London to set up house and form a band with three old schoolmates. Being strapped for beer money whilst waiting for the royalty cheques to turn up, I went looking for some temporary work and was offered a few weeks' work as an accounts clerk with the British Airports Authority (now simply BAA).

Twelve months later, the band folded. I'd like to pretend it was for personal and musical reasons, but the truth is that we preferred playing bridge to rehearsing. Twelve years later, I was BAA's Training and Development Manager at Gatwick Airport. In the intervening period, I drifted into a permanent accounts job and then took an internal transfer into personnel. Within days of starting in that department – it might even have been hours come to think of it – I was 'encouraged' to pursue a professional qualification. The rewards looked good and personnel looked like a reasonably comfortable area to stay in.

Once I was qualified, it seemed perverse to move anywhere else. I was earning a decent salary that I felt I wouldn't be able to match anywhere else given that I would have dropped to the bottom rung of a new career structure. Eighteen years after the band broke up, I was a mildly disillusioned HR professional. Somewhere along the line, I had forgotten to ask myself what I really wanted to do.

When I finally got round to facing my career demons, it became increasingly apparent that corporate life and I needed to go our separate ways. Within a matter of a few months, I'd left

There's more on putting together a functional CV in IDEA 6, *What's your type?*

Try another idea...

my job and set myself up as a self-employed change consultant, career counsellor, writer, associate university lecturer, and CD and record seller.

Since that time, my CV has been in mothballs. I've advised thousands of people about their CVs, I've helped on a variety of recruitment exercises and I've researched and written extensively on the subject, but I've had no personal need for one.

Now I imagine you're wondering why I'm telling you all this. Well, I simply want to make the point that not all careers beg for CVs to underpin them and to drive them forward. The world is full of people who manage perfectly well without one, including many an artist, sculptor, musician, aromatherapist, street vendor, builder, plumber, sandwich maker, basket weaver, bicycle repairer, magician, etc. However, even if you don't have a CV and don't anticipate needing one in the future because your next work is more likely to come about through a contact or a recommendation, don't entirely let go of the possibility that one day you might just need a CV. If that day ever comes and you need to produce one for the first time in years, then you'll really wish you'd kept a running note of what you've been up to, the things you've done in your working life that you're proud of and the dates you did them.

So, consider keeping an ongoing record of what you get up to, just as I've been doing all this time.

'Some of the most wonderful people are the ones who don't fit into boxes.'
TORI AMOS, writer and singer

Defining idea...

How did it go?

Q I've decided that I don't want a conventional career after all and that I'm going to set up a business renovating banjos. Does this mean that I can pass this book to my nephew?

A *You're clearly somebody who doesn't fit into a box, in which case you might go years without giving your CV a second look. On the other hand, are you certain that you'll never need it again? If there's the slightest chance that you might, I really would commend noting down what you get up to and when.*

Q OK, I'll take your advice. Any other parting shots?

A *If you do end up having to put a CV together after many years in an unconventional career, you'll almost certainly find that the functional CV is the one to go with. This particular format emphasises your skills and competencies as opposed to recent job history and experience. And that's precisely what you'll need to do if the appeal of the banjo should ever wear thin.*

51

Treat your CV as a vade mecum

The dictionary definition of 'vade mecum' is 'a handbook or other aid carried on the person for immediate use when needed.' Here are the benefits of owning one.

Whatever we choose to do with our careers, one thing is certain: the job for life has been pensioned off.

According to Thomas Stewart, author of *Intellectual Capital*, these days 'you have a better chance of getting a gold watch from a street vendor than you do from a corporation'. Companies lose money and they purge staff. Companies announce record profits and they purge staff. Let's face it, the concept of a one-company career, as understood by generations of workers before us, is dead and gone.

These days, the very idea that an individual can join a company from school or college and work their way up from office junior to president of the company seems ridiculous. Anyway, can any of us be confident that our employer will be around long enough to underwrite that form of stately progression to the top?

Here's an idea for you... **Develop a 'personal recovery plan' to enable you to cope more effectively in the event of your job/primary source of income disappearing tomorrow. What would you do? How would you pay the rent/mortgage? Is this an opportunity for a career change?**

If you think the fact that your current employer gave you a job means that they value and appreciate you, you may need to think again. A survey in 1999 from the Institute of Directors and Development Dimensions International asked HR directors what percentage of their employees they'd rehire if they could change all their employees overnight. Half said they'd rehire between 0% and 40%.

So, 21st-century organisations only want us if we're a source of 'added value'. Or to put it another way, we're entering an era of conditional corporate love. We'd therefore do well to make sure that our CV is never too far from our grasp, as who knows when we might need it next.

There's more to this than simply storing a copy of your CV on a floppy disk labelled 'For emergency use only'. You need to have an attitude towards your CV and career that shouts to the world that you're in charge. You've made a good start in looking for help here, but it's not enough. To tweak a cliché: today is the first day of the rest of your career. So what are you going to do about it? Here are a few tips for thriving in today's uncertain corporate climate:

Defining idea... **'When there's nothing you can learn where you are, you've got to move on, even if they give you promotions.'**
JOHN KOTTER, Harvard Business School professor

Keep your CV bang up to date: Maintain an ongoing record of new experience, achievements and qualifications gained. There's always a risk that important information will slip from your mind if you don't note it down while it's still fresh. Also, keep an eye out for other people's CVs so that you're in touch with the latest CV fashions.

> Don't let your network fall into a state of disrepair. Head back to IDEA 43, *Networking*.

Try another idea...

Don't entrust your career to anybody: Relying on the Chief Executive, your boss or the Management Development Manager to look after your career interests is a touchingly naive but fatally flawed strategy. They have other fish to fry.

Be visible: Find ways to raise your profile. Network like crazy.

Develop career purpose: People with a vision of their futures, and goals linked to that vision, are far more likely to succeed than those who don't.

Think ahead: Taking care of your job isn't the same as taking care of your career. To avoid career inertia, schedule in regular reviews of where you and your career are heading and consciously set out to acquire new skills and knowledge.

Be flexible: Have an overall sense of direction, but be ready to improvise.

> *'I never make predictions. I never have and I never will.'*
> TONY BLAIR, as quoted on a greetings card

Defining idea...

Q **I'm fed up with all this nanosecond noughties stuff telling me that the job for life is dead. Are things really all that different?**

A   *The average length of time we spend in a job has remained pretty constant over the past twenty years. Companies are making fewer people redundant. But the job market itself has changed significantly. Twenty-five years ago, 75% of people of working age were in full-time permanent jobs; nowadays that figure is nearer half. In the intervening years, we've seen a sizeable growth in part-time work, temporary work and the number of people who are self-employed. Our relationship with the workplace has indeed changed to the point where having a decent quality CV to hand seems like an eminently sensible precaution.*

Q **Do I really need to have a Personal Recovery Plan as you suggest?**

A   *You don't necessarily need a formal bound document that sets out in writing how you might respond to different scenarios that fate might hurl at you. However, we're a generation of workers who have taken on levels of financial commitment that our parents could only begin to imagine, and to the point where many of us will have real difficulty coping if our source of income goes. Given that, a bit of forward thinking really doesn't seem out of place.*

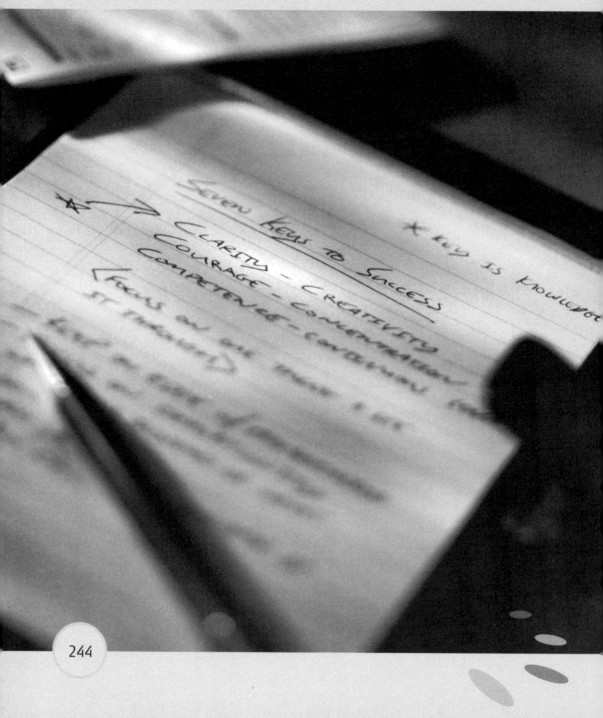

52

One last thing (20 actually)

Use this checklist to ensure that you send your CV out in a fit state.

Let's assume that you've absorbed what you will from the previous 51 ideas, seen the job of your dreams and had a crack at putting together a CV that will blow the recruiter's socks off.

Just before you seal your CV in the envelope and head off to the postbox, why not refer to this 20-item checklist that is intended to help reassure you that your CV is as good as it could be. See how yours measures up in its current state.

1. Have you researched the role you're applying for as well as you possibly can? Is your research reflected in the content of your CV?

2. Double-check that all your contact details are up to date. Make sure you've given a mobile number and your email address. If your email is something like fluffybunnyinboobooland362436@hotmail.com, consider changing it for something that sounds a tad more professional.

Here's an idea for you... **Make a list of your career priorities for the next six months. Then put an entry in your diary for six months from today, marking it something like 'Personal Review', and on that date allow yourself at least a couple of hours to take stock of how you got on. Make this an ongoing process.**

3. Does your profile statement explicitly target the role you're applying for?

4. Have you provided evidence to back up anything you've said about yourself in your profile?

5. Have you quantified the information in your CV as much as possible?

6. Have you put your achievements in order of relevance and significance to fit the job you're applying for?

7. Have you used terminology that people outside your present company will understand?

8. Check that you've avoided jargon, acronyms and abbreviations where possible.

9. Does your CV look balanced? Have you put most emphasis on your most recent career with diminishing levels of detail as you go back in time to earlier roles? Remember that corporate pre-history began about six years ago.

9. Does your CV sound upbeat? Does it read as though you are enthusiastic about tackling the role?

10. Are you confident that you could talk through any aspect of your CV if it came up at an interview? Eliminate any content that you may feel uncomfortable discussing rather than creating a hostage to fortune.

> **Close your eyes and pick a page, any page. Whichever idea you alight on, it *will* be relevant.**

Try another idea...

11. Double-check any dates. There are a surprising number of CVs in circulation where people managed to start a job in 2003 and leave it in 2001.

12. Make sure that you have given the reference for the job you are applying for and where you saw that advert.

13. Have you provided all the information that the advertisement specified, such as salary details, dates available for interview, etc.?

14. Check for typos. Sounds obvious I know, but it's so easy to let a phew slip though the net. Don't rely on your software package's spellchecker – the number of senior 'mangers' that show up on CVs is staggering.

> *'Successful job hunting is a learned skill. You have to study it. You have to practise it. You have to master it, just like any new skill. And master it thoroughly because you'll need it all the rest of your life.'*
> RICHARD BOLLES, careers guru and author of *What Color Is Your Parachute?*

Defining idea...

247

15. Have you used good-quality paper and a good printer for your CV and covering letter? If it's an application form, have you completed it in black ink to ensure that it will photocopy well?

16. Have you asked somebody to look through your CV?

17. Put your application into an A4 envelope and send it out by first-class post.

18. Feel free to add anything to the checklist that strikes you as helpful.

19. If you haven't been doing so already, from now on keep an ongoing note of your achievements at work and any job changes so that you're prepared for when you next need to go through this entire process.

20. I think that's about it. Good luck! Let me know how you get on.

How did it go?

Q **I've just handed in my notice to my current employers. Do you have any tips on exiting with style?**

A   *When it comes to handing in your notice, remember that the way we leave a company speaks volumes about us. So leave with good grace: buy the doughnuts and maybe a round of drinks; go around the office and personally say goodbye to the people you liked as well as any others who you'd like to speak well of you; and whatever you do, don't lace any* farewell speeches with vitriol – you're not going to endear yourself to your soon-to-be former colleagues by telling them what mugs they are for staying there.

Q **Tomorrow is my first day in my new job. How should I play things?**

A Bear in mind that your new boss, colleagues and team, possibly the whole organisation, will be watching you in the early days. First impressions count. Here are a few tips on how to prolong the honeymoon period:

Be visible. Get out and meet as many people as possible.

Find out who's who, get to grips with company polices and procedures. Absorb as much as you can as quickly as you can.

Don't refer to your former organisation as 'we'; in fact, only ever refer to your past experience if it's relevant in some way.

Be guarded about your views. There will be plenty of organisational hot potatoes and people will be trying to recruit you to their various causes or grievances.

Make something happen as soon as you can. If 100 days have gone by and the impression people have got is that little if anything has changed, then you've missed a trick.

Bonus ideas

1

Please Sir, can I have some more?

Salary is an important component of your brilliant career. It also defines one of the main boundaries of your lifestyle. Negotiate for more when the time is ripe. Make sure you are being paid at least what you are worth and preferably a bit more.

NEVER tell anyone your salary. Whatever you say will do you or them no good. Either it will be less than they thought, which diminishes their respect, or it will be more than they either expect or think you are worth. This leads to jealousy.

Keep the big picture in view. Particularly at the start of your career, keep in mind that the rewards of getting to the top are very substantial. Don't whinge about your early salary. Tell yourself that you are investing for the future. Agree to small or no rises and even no promotions for the first couple of years, then go for the big hike when you have something to argue with.

Here's an idea for you... **By using recruitment agencies, the internet and the HR department you should be able to work out the top and bottom ends of the sort of salary someone in your position gets. Now work out why you deserve to be in the top 25% of the band. When you have a good case, take it to your boss. If you are already in the top quartile, look for a promotion.**

You might be better off doing an extra few months at 20k a year rather than causing grief by bellyaching. The eventual return could be well worth it.

I was working in a theatre once when an assistant stage manager did a bunk with the £100 she had been given to buy props. 'What a mug,' said a more seasoned ASM, 'If she had waited a bit longer she could have gone off with five times that.' So it is in business. It's only the people with no vision who fiddle their expenses for a couple of pints in the pub, or charge for a first-class train fare and sit in second. This is short sighted in many ways. After all, who do you need to impress who sits in standard class?

IT'S A LOT ABOUT TIMING

When you are going into a new job make sure that they really want you to join them and preferably have told other contenders that the job is not theirs before negotiating the salary. Asking earlier has two disadvantages. First, you may discover that there is a big gap between their expectations and yours. At that time you are negotiating from a position of weakness, since they have not yet decided if they want you. Second, it makes you look a bit small if the salary is the only reason you're taking the job.

Whatever anyone tells you, you can ask for more money at any time. The key here is timing: ask when your value to the organisation appears very high. Do it when you have just brought off a big deal, or organised the district conference or made a useful suggestion for change. Focus on what you have done and what you will do in the future. Use simple techniques of negotiation like the 'It's only 10 a week rather than 520 a year.'

The same timing works when you're looking for a promotion. Think, act and look as though you are already in the new job. Seek out, and go after, vacancies. I was managing a small sales team in Scotland when the manager of a large team in a higher job category got a promotion. As soon as I heard the news I telephoned his boss, whom I knew, and asked for the job. I think he was simply saving the time and stress of interviewing when he agreed.

'The salary of the Chief Executive of the large corporation is not a market reward for achievement. It is frequently in the nature of a warm personal gesture from the person to him or her self.'
J.K. GALBRAITH, American economist

Defining idea...

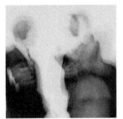

How did it go?

Q   Is it possible to get over the company policy that salaries are only reviewed once a year?

A   *Normally yes, and certainly in very many cases. If you've increased your worth over the last twelve months, combine this enhanced status with a hint of unfairness. In terms of unfairness it is probably best to avoid the straight 'But they're earning more than me.' Do it more subtly.*

Q   I think I am underpaid and am going to look for a new job if they don't do something about it. Should I tell them?

A   *If you use it as a gun to their head, you reduce the value equation and represent only a threat. It's generally not good news. The boldest way would be to get another job and then tell them that you have a real intention to move if they don't come up with the goods.*

This idea originally appeared in *Cultivate a cool career: Guerilla tactics for reaching the top* by Ken Langdon.

2

So, why do you want this job?

Turn a question like this into a selling opportunity by using a double answer – balance what you'll get out of the job with what they'll get out of hiring you.

It should be reasonably easy to answer this one as long as you're going for the right job. If it's very difficult, then ask yourself if this is the right employer for you before you go in.

An employer wants people to join them with enthusiasm for the challenges they're about to face. Similarly you want to get into an environment where your working life gives you joy rather than grief. Research and good self-insight will give you the right answer to achieve both aims.

WHAT'S IN IT FOR ME?

It's probably best to start the dual answer with the straightforward answer to the question. It's another question that depends on your research. You've got to be able to reply in terms of the company's attributes as you find them. It doesn't really matter what the situation is; you can still paint it as ideal for you. 'Most people want to work for the market leader; I could use your name with pride' could

Here's an idea for you... **This question really is one to prepare for carefully. The time will never be wasted, since this question will always crop up in one way or other. The best way to prepare is to find someone to role-play the interviewer and then try out with them the actual words you're going to use. If you can get someone in the same industry that would be best, but anyone with good experience of organisations or business should be able to help.**

equally be, 'I like the way you've made such progress in your industry over the last few years. A growing company like yours suits my energetic way of working. I really enjoy success.'

Now try to get in something about their reputation. 'I understand that you can offer me a stable, challenging and inspiring work environment – you certainly have that reputation. I think it's the sort of environment that brings out the best in me.'

Now compliment the company on what it actually does. 'Many people regard your products and services as the best around. It's a pride thing again; I like to work for someone who is passionate about service and quality. I think we share those values and that I would enjoy fitting into your team.'

AND WHAT'S IN IT FOR THEM?

Your unique selling proposition is you and your skills and experience. Try to work out a way of illustrating that everything you've done points at you being the right person for them. Perhaps start from specific experience. For a team leader in credit control: 'My experience in the credit control department of a builders' merchants was, frankly, a hard school. The building industry is always suffering from companies going under. I know about collection periods, credit ratings calculated from company reports and, of course, I've heard every excuse under the sun for not being quite ready to issue the cheque. I think that as team leader I would be able to help others to learn from that experience.'

Now relate the specific skills to the goals of the organisation. 'I understand the benefits to you of getting payment in on time or even before time because I've controlled cash flow for an organisation and seen the impact it can have on profitability.'

You can also be more open about your skills where you're sure they're appropriate. For a production manager: 'I've always scored well in problem solving and from what you've said you need to find some new ways of cutting down the waste at the end of the production line.'

Something more personal can emphasise your uniqueness. For a training deliverer: 'The fact that I've done a bit of amateur dramatics helps me to understand the "performance" side of running a training course.'

Now bring the three things together: 'So you see why I was excited when I saw your job ad; you seem to need a person with pretty much the experience, skills and interests that I've developed.'

'And so my fellow Americans: ask not what your country can do for you – ask what you can do for your country.'
JOHN F. KENNEDY

Defining idea...

How did it go?

Q   **I've thought long and hard about this. There's rather a good job in a company that's not doing very well. I think part of the problem is that their values don't include a focus on teamwork. They have a reputation for 'hire and fire' and come over as a bit 'every man for themselves.' When they ask this question should I point out that while I'm not sure I share their current values I think I can introduce some new ones that will help to improve their performance?**

A   *Possibly. Our first reaction to this was 'NO, wait until you've got the job and then sell the changes that you think they need to make.' But on second thoughts you could be right. Depends if you think that someone in the room is thinking the same way as you, in which case go for it. You could get the pleasant surprise of one of them telling you that they know they need to change in this area – in which case your preparation is ideal. (Sorry to be sceptical, but you should also bear in mind the words in script font at the top of this Idea.)*

Q   **I'd like to end this answer with a bold statement. Can I say that I would like to be in my boss's position within two years – in order to demonstrate my ambition?**

A   *Yes, but choose the words carefully. You're trying to make them feel confident about you, not insecure. Try, 'Finally, I have aspirations to get to your level in the not too distant future.'*

This idea originally appeared in *Knockout interview answers: 52 brilliant ideas to make job hunting a piece of cake* by Ken Langdon and Nikki Cartwright.

3

All time is playtime

If it's daytime it must be playtime. Work out how every interaction of the day can be 'played'.

People who turn everything into a game are often portrayed as wily operators, or supercilious types who don't really take anything seriously.

But nearly every interaction you have in the world is something of a game – in most cases, you just haven't worked the rules out yet.

Gameplayers have a lot to teach us about exposing the basic working parts of any experience and identifying its creative value. If you can learn to master the 'rules' of any given situation, often it means that you can 'play' that situation more creatively each time it occurs. Not only are you staying alert to the creative potential of the moment, you're honing your critical and emotional responses. Like every good sports player, you're engaged in a programme of intensive training. And by making things hyper-real in this way, you're becoming hyper-sensitive to your surroundings.

What we're describing here is not unlike what happens to you the first time you put on a portable music player and go walking around a big city. Suddenly your life

Here's an idea for you... **Constantly analyse your action, to become more self-aware. Thinking of even the most inane tasks as training can allow you to perceive value in them. When you poured yourself a coffee or tea this morning, did you do it 'better' than yesterday? Was your pouring action smooth? Did you pour from a greater height? Was there any spillage? It sounds silly, but an Olympic pole vaulter will be asking these kinds of questions every time he or she trains (not about coffee-pouring, obviously).**

has a soundtrack and you feel like you're acting in a movie. Perhaps you start to walk like John Travolta. Every passer-by is potentially another actor in your movie. Every moment is pregnant with the possibility of being a 'big scene'. Try it and see how it changes your perception of what you thought was a familiar landscape. Try walking the same route to two radically different soundtracks and see what kind of emotions and thoughts each one elicits.

In the last couple of years, digital artists such as Blast Theory have taken this idea one step further by developing ways of playing an online role-playing game even as you carry on your normal life around town – as portayed in their project *Uncle Roy All Around You* (for details of how to play, go to www.uncleroyallaroundyou.co.uk). When you take part in games like these you definitely look at everything with fresh eyes and lose your complacency about everday existence. Suddenly everything that happens has to fit in with your sense of the game, and thus every experience takes on a new sense.

In a way, many people are already doing something similar in their lives by not only adding a soundtrack to the day with iPods and Walkmans, but using mobile text messaging to communicate with 'players', setting themselves 'missions' throughout the day, acquiring 'kit' and winning 'powers' or 'rewards'. All the basic ingredients of a PlayStation game like *Tomb Raider* or *Splinter Cell* are there. (Getting to know your way around a PlayStation is *de rigueur* for creative people these days, by the way.)

'Life must be lived as play.'
PLATO

Defining idea...

Try now to map out a typical day of yours as if it were a console game. You may well reveal patterns that you hadn't seen before. Perhaps a new soundtrack will emerge. You may also find that you achieve more distance from events in which you're usually immersed. By seeing it all as a game, you can stay above it all and therefore learn to be more dispassionate about assessing the value of various experiences.

Getting better at games, of course, requires practice and repetition. You may think that you've already got enough routine and repetition in your life, and you may feel hemmed in or bored by it. But ultimately you'll gain an instinctive understanding of such high falutin' concepts as 'flow' and 'immersion' – those moments in both games and real life when you feel completely at ease in terms of your concentration, your awareness, your appreciation, your instincts, physical ability and skill level; in fact, exactly the kind of feeling you want others to have when they're immersed in something you've created.

How did it go?

Q **Most games, particularly computer games, seem to be based around solving puzzles of one kind or another. I spend my life problem solving and I hate puzzles, so why should I be interested in games?**

A   *We're not asking you to fill up your leisure time playing games (well, maybe just a bit). What we're suggesting is more fundamental, with the emphasis on 'fun'. Trying to reorganise your creative process so that it becomes more game-like, by inventing arbitrary rules, for example, is what you should aim for. If you enjoy what you do, chances are other people will enjoy it too.*

Q **Playing games just makes me better at games. My creative life hasn't changed at all. Why not?**

A   *Well, we'd claim you're just not paying attention to what's going on when you're playing games. Here are some pointers that poker player and writer Larry W. Phillips feels can be taken from the card table and applied to life:*

1. take the long view
2. once you commit to a hand, play it strong
3. don't throw in good money after bad
4. if you think you're beat, get out.

This idea originally appeared in *Unleash your creativity: 52 brilliant ideas for creative genius* by Rob Bevan and Tim Wright.

264

The end...

Or is it a new beginning?

We hope that you've been inspired to revamp your résumé. Now when you send your CV to your next employer you'll know it's going to hit the spot precisely. Let us know if it really works. We'd love to hear your stories.

If there was an idea that you struggled to understand, tell us about that too. Tell us how you got on generally. What did it for you – which were the tips that helped you to craft a really punchy CV? Maybe you've got some tips of your own that you want to share. If you liked this book you may find we have more brilliant ideas for other areas that could help change your life for the better.

You'll find the Infinite Ideas crew waiting for you online at www.infideas.com.

Or if you prefer to write, then send your letters to:
High Impact CVs
The Infinite Ideas Company Ltd
36 St Giles, Oxford, OX1 3LD, United Kingdom

We want to know what you think, because we're all working on making our lives better too. Give us your feedback and you could win a copy of another *52 Brilliant Ideas* book of your choice. Or maybe get a crack at writing your own.

Good luck. Be brilliant.

Offer one

CASH IN YOUR IDEAS

We hope you enjoy this book. We hope it inspires, amuses, educates and entertains you. But we don't assume that you're a novice, or that this is the first book that you've bought on the subject. You've got ideas of your own. Maybe our author has missed an idea that you use successfully. If so, why not send it to yourauthormissedatrick@infideas.com, and if we like it we'll post it on our bulletin board. Better still, if your idea makes it into print we'll send you four books of your choice or the cash equivalent. You'll be fully credited so that everyone knows you've had another Brilliant Idea.

Offer two

HOW COULD YOU REFUSE?

Amazing discounts on bulk quantities of Infinite Ideas books are available to corporations, professional associations and other organisations.

For details call us on:
+44 (0)1865 514888
Fax: +44 (0)1865 514777
or e-mail: info@infideas.com

Where it's at...

Brilliant discounts on professional CV writing services

jobs direct from employers

≡ FULLER CV
creating your richer future

Did you know that a single job can attract more than 1000 CVs?
Yet only one interview is granted for every 50–100 CVs received by the average employer.
Scared? It gets worse – 75–80% of CVs are not even read beyond the first page!

So outshine the competition and take advantage of a **15% discount** on professional CV writing services from **The Fuller CV** and **workthing.com**. Then simply upload your CV onto the UK's largest network of specialist jobsites, www.workthing.com to get your CV in front of the best employer brands in the UK.

Career Consultants at The Fuller CV are seasoned professionals, with experience working in vertical markets, together with extensive recruitment expertise. They typically hold professional memberships including those of the Institute of Personnel and Development and Recruitment and Employment Confederation. Advice is therefore built upon solid foundations and their mission is to work with you to provide compelling career tools for your future success.

By registering with workthing.com your CV will be immediately accessible for their direct employers as well as accessible by all advertisers across their specialist network.

So what are you waiting for? To take advantage of the Fuller CV service call **01932 836700***
today and quote 'workthing offer' to obtain your 15% discount.

*Normal national and international telephone rates apply.

brilliant ideas

High impact CVs is published by Infinite Ideas, publishers of the acclaimed **52 Brilliant Ideas** series. With the **52 Brilliant Ideas** series you can enhance your existing skills or knowledge with negligible investment of time or money and can substantially improve your performance or know-how of a subject over the course of a year. Or day. Or month. The choice is yours. There are more than 45 titles published in subject areas as diverse as: health & relationships; sports, hobbies & games; lifestyle & leisure and careers, finance & personal development. To learn more, to join our mailing list or to find out about discounts and special offers visit www.infideas.com, or e-mail info@infideas.com.